The Liberating Beauty of Little Things

Decision, Adversity & Reckoning in a Refugee's Journey from Prague to Cambridge

BOHUSLAVA BRADBROOK

THE Alpha PRESS

BRIGHTON • PORTLAND

2 4 6 8 10 9 7 5 3 1
First published 2000 in Great Britain by
THE ALPHA PRESS
Box 2950
Brighton BN2 5SP

and in the United States of America by
THE ALPHA PRESS
5804 N.E. Hassalo St.
Portland, Oregon 97213-3644

British Library Cataloguing in Publication Data
A CIP catalogue record for this book is available from the British Library.

Library of Congress Cataloging-in-Publication Data
Bradbrook, B. R.
The liberating beauty of little things ; decision, adversity & reckoning in a refugee's journey from Prague to Cambridge / Bohuslava R. Bradbrook.
p. cm.
ISBN 1–898595–34–8 (alk. paper)
1. Bradbrook, B. R. 2. Refugees—Czechoslovakia—Biography. 3. Czechs—England.
4. Czechoslovakia—Emigration and immigration—History—20th century. 5. England—Emigration and immigration—History—20th century. I. Title.
DB2221.B73 A3 2000
304.8′420437′09045—dc21   00–061103

Printed by Bookcraft, Midsomer Norton, Bath
This book is printed on acid-free paper

THE LIBERATING BEAUTY OF LITTLE THINGS
Decision, Adversity & Reckoning in a Refugee's Journey from
Prague to Cambridge

To Sandy and family,
with love and best wishes.
from
Bohumil q.

To the Memory of
Muriel
and all the Members of my Czech Family
who suffered for me.

Contents

Preface

As one grows older, perhaps it is natural to look back and ask what turn our lives would have taken if we had acted differently in vital situations in the past. Imagine a common, young and hopeful person living in Central Europe in the middle of the twentieth century, trapped in political turmoil and confronted, all of a sudden, with unexpected adversities. What can the individual do? Just when such a person looks forward to a new, settled life, reaping the fruit of earlier labour, the realization dawns as to how much freedom and human rights are being violated and the high price that would have to be paid to liberate oneself from such a predicament.

The Czech modern classic writer Karel Čapek wrote about "the liberating beauty of little things", which often brought him relief as he could see the comic side of tense, stressful situations. I hope that many refugees from my native Czechoslovakia (now the Czech Republic) were heartened similarly on their thorny ways into exile.

In my lifetime there were three waves of refugees. The first were those fleeing from Hitler in various ways; the third sought asylum after the Russian invasion of Czechoslovakia in 1968, if they happened to be visiting Western countries at the time; the second, to which I belong, left their country after the communist *putsch* in 1948, during the few following years before the Iron Curtain became impenetrable. Most of these refugees just walked out, "over the hills". The phrase, then used, indicated the illegal crossing of the frontier to the Western part of Europe. In my case, however, "the hills" were the river Dyje which forms a natural frontier between Moravia and Austria.

I committed the most important events of this memoir to paper a few years after my escape, lest I forget them; but by the time I sat down to write this book, I had forgotten the names of many individuals who shared my story. Where possible, I have used real names

– many individuals who feature here are well-known people; those who are nameless or for whom I invent names in this memoir, remain alive in my memory, but I have lost touch with them during those long years. Most of them no longer live, but in any case, if there are those who can still recognize themselves, I trust that they will not find anything of offense in my truthful story.

I have used the term "refugees" as we were called then. How much more promising the newer designation "asylum seekers" sounds! It is very sad that they still exist. They seem to be coming in alarmingly large numbers, by public transport, often with passports and money, appearing uninvited on the doorsteps of their chosen countries – yet, frustrated, fearful and unhappy. The prosperous Western countries have to protect their own homelands against abuses of their hospitality, for asylum abusers are to be found among the asylum seekers. But if we cannot tolerate genuine political refugees, how then can we even tolerate each other?

It would be wise to remember how we might look and behave to others if we were suddenly uprooted from our homes, and placed in foreign circumstances with little money, an over-bearing bureaucracy, and fear of personal and familial reprisal in the land one escaped from. Humility is a small word with a big meaning. Putting this memoir to paper has reminded me of that.

Decision

Chapter I

Prague 1952
driven into a narrow corner
looking back to war years
the liberation, 1945
the fatal February 1948 and its consequences

So, the ceremony was over. The majestic statue of the Emperor Charles IV who founded the Prague University in 1348 towered over me in the large hall of the Carolinum as I held the scroll containing my Ph.D. diploma, but this precious object was soon obliterated in my arms as they were filled by bunches of flowers from well-wishers. No, no other presents were habitual then (1952), neither was there a special party for the family and friends to follow, as for most of us such luxury was beyond our means. Through the post-war devaluation of the currency our savings were written off, except for a small allowance to students during their first degree studies. Mine, in Czech and English, was a four-year course, with qualifications for grammar school teaching on completion, but a research degree was considered non-essential, so that we had to earn our living throughout the extra period of study. What other than private tutorship was compatible with the long hours needed for the work in the University Library?

Now, this was all over. The hard research work, the tension before the rigorous oral examinations, as well as the endless rushing through Prague streets from one pupil to another. The feeling of relief was tremendous, but was I really free? On my graduation day I wanted to forget that private teaching would not be adequate indefinitely and, moreover, would not be permissible in a communist régime; everyone had to have a proper job, that is, full-time and in a state-run institution, so that each individual could be under control. In my optimism I tried not to believe that my chances of a good post would be hampered by my resistance to join the communist party or toe the party line. Perhaps I would be lucky again to slip through the net, as happened to me during those horrible student purges in 1948 when masses of non-conforming students were forced to leave university, while others were spared, probably on the basis of their good academic record, or just sheer good luck? Little did I realize that, four years later, toeing the party line became the essential requisite for any enterprise.

By now, people could feel the full extent of the political oppression. With my graduation over, the true reality hit me hard. I saw that intellectual work was valued very little; the glorification of menial work degraded it to the lowest level, as the few openings were reserved only for those perhaps less well qualified but prepared to conform with the Marxist ideology. After nearly seven years of honest study which I enjoyed, was I to end in a factory or perhaps, at best, among teachers, exposed to continual control, spied on, always afraid of being dismissed? Obviously, if I were accepted as a teacher, it would be only a matter of time before I would be dismissed and degraded. Occasionally among friends in a similar situation, we would try to cheer ourselves up by quoting or inventing political jokes and anecdotes, ridiculing the régime and its leaders; it was the only, small, ineffective vindictive measure we could take. This flourished during the Nazi occupation, too, but petered out soon afterwards, just as now we hear no more of those jokes dating from the communist era. Obviously, they did bring some relief from oppression: why did we not need them in my young days, in the first Czechoslovak Republic?

The thought of the early part of my life, spent in that free country, makes me very nostalgic. Its democracy, modelled on the West European states, allowed us to speak and act freely, there was no need to invent vindictive jokes to lift our hearts; anecdotes about President T. G. Masaryk were endearing rather than derogatory: his exemplary life of integrity and high moral values would have disarmed potential critics. The country may have been small and not very rich in comparison with its West European neighbours – the recession in the thirties hit it just the same as elsewhere, but our culture flourished, the spirit of freedom kept together the nation for whom there appeared to be a promising future.

Yes, the sense of freedom is inborn to all creatures great and small; if one is born and bred in a democratic country, a foreign yoke feels twice as heavy and doubles one's wish to shake it off. If this proves impossible, only an escape remains. Yet, who would like to leave one's home? I do not mean leaving it for a few years to study in the capital or take a temporary post abroad – I mean for an indefinite, very uncertain period, perhaps for good, never to be allowed to return?

Although my father died when I was only three, so that my mother had to bring up my brother (nine years older) and myself on a considerably restricted budget, our small family lived a contented, harmonious life, not very different from British middle-class families in similar circumstances. My brother's departure in the thirties from our home in Moravia for university studies in Prague did not loosen our close loving relationship; we felt secure in the belief that honest work would be rewarded on its true merit. But the Munich agreement in 1938 changed all.

The day after the tragic verdict, my school friend and I mounted our bicycles to go and visit our Czech friends living in the area of the dispute, because soon they would be part of Germany. A few days later we saw our demobilized army returning home, humiliated and downcast, because they were not allowed to defend their homeland. A few Jewish classmates disappeared: we had no idea that they were the lucky ones who escaped to the Middle East or some free country in Western Europe or the United States. They were soon replaced in the school by many new arrivals whose parents preferred to sacrifice their properties in the occupied territories and moved to the Czech mainland, the parts of it which were left to the Czechs. Accommodation and jobs had to be found for these refugees; chaos and uncertainty prevailed, especially when the Poles and the Hungarians, too, claimed their piece of the cake and more refugees from those parts also moved further inland.

The German army marched into Bohemia and Moravia in March 1939, just on my birthday. Slush was spluttering under their feet on this grey day; shops and restaurants were soon empty, the hospital full of greedy (or hungry?) sick soldiers who had eaten too much too quickly. What was going to happen was anybody's guess, but the sabre-rattling sounded ominous. When the war broke out, most of the Jewish population – not very large in our town of some 20,000 inhabitants –– unsuspecting, stayed in their homes, as it was beyond anybody's imagination to foresee what was in store for them. Our Jewish schoolmates ceased to attend school; public transport was forbidden them and if they were seen walking in the street, yellow stars were shining on the lapels or sleeves of their outer garments. Young and ignorant as I was, I ran one day in public to greet my friend Alice: "Oh, please, please, don't talk to me, I can't answer, I'm not allowed to speak to anyone!" she whispered, full of anxiety, and quickly disappeared. In my youthful complacent optimism I refused to believe the prophecy of my Jewish teacher of German, that the war was going to last for six years. How did she know? For a while I continued taking my German lessons in her home; although scared that she might suffer if someone saw me visiting her, the lady was glad to have some contact with the outside world. When eventually all the Jews were moved to a guarded ghetto, a large house not far from the town centre, they were almost completely cut off. Their tiny food ration coupons could not be redeemed before 4 p.m. when shops were already empty; and they were not allowed to cross the town boundary where, on the outskirts, they could buy some vegetables from the market gardeners. Only the darkness of the blackout could hide the basket of vegetables deposited on their doorstep; the doorbell brought about its quick disappearance, while I was hiding round the corner to collect the empty basket ten minutes later. Thump, thump, I heard the heavy boots of the guard as did the people inside the house, too. Then, one day, the basket was left, not emptied, on the doorstep of the dark, now empty house. I did not see my teacher, or any other of the house's occupants, again.

But gentile members of the community were disappearing, too. Already on 17 November 1939 university students in Prague, provoked by the shooting of their medical colleague Jan Opletal, staged a protest march; most of them were arrested to swell considerably the population of the concentration camp in Oranienburg near Berlin. But this punishment was not enough: the Nazis closed all Czech universities instantly and they would not be reopened until after the war. German universities would have accepted these stranded Czech students (not imprisoned), but the offer came like an insult rather than an attractive gesture to them. After a long time one of my friends returned from Oranienburg; pale, with cheeks puffed up after the treatment by bromine, designed to make them look well fed. He was unusually silent.

Broadcasts from the West were forbidden to us, but the cage into which our country was crammed became even tighter when the "doctoring" of our radios was ordered. We had to take them to the town hall where short-wave bands were officially removed. Not many radio amateurs had the knowledge or material to make their own replacements to insert and remove them according to need; yet, some information reached us from time to time, in spite of the fact that the death penalty could have been imposed on those who were caught listening. What a relief to hear from this source that two of my uncles who would have been thorns in the Nazi's flesh were safely in London! Sadly, we waited in vain to hear something similar about one of my cousins, a young budding poet, who also disappeared from our midst. He perished in the Mauthausen concentration camp – smothered to death by chairs, as one of the camp survivors later told us.

Some time in the middle of the war tragedy hit our town. A young man whom we had not seen for some time, fell to his death after his parachute failed to open. He was found in the neighbouring wood. We thought that he was safe somewhere in Britain – which was true until he volunteered to be flown back by the military on a mission as a parachutist. Sad enough that this gifted young man was dead, but his love for his former girl friend (who felt free after his escape from the country and now had another boyfriend) led to a further disaster. Her photograph in his pocket provided identity links for the Nazis, leading to the immediate execution of both families involved: the girlfriend, four parents, his brother and his pregnant wife – only the very young sister of the girlfriend survived, sheltered by nuns in a convent.

In 1942, after the assassination of the Reichsprotector Heidrich, such instantaneous executions occurred daily. As if the vengeful burning down of Lidice and Ležáky with the deaths of all the male population was not enough, the Nazis were determined to exterminate our cultural élite. Every day a number of intellectuals, artists, writers or any prominent personalities were taken and shot the same day. I cannot remember how long this went on, but the execution of the Mayor of Prague with a number of others stands clearly in my mind, as it happened on my brother's wedding day.

By now I had qualified as a teacher after having finished a specialist grammar school/teacher training course. As our universities were closed, only private endeavour could lead to higher qualifications, in languages and music in my case. Teachers were in short supply and, soon enough, I found myself teaching at a secondary modern type of school in my native town. Not for long, though, as novices to the job were expected to fill vacancies of greatest needs; this meant changing schools more frequently than the older colleagues had to, and commuting within the area of the inspectorate. Life was too uncertain for anyone to leave one's home and rent rooms (if these happened to be available) in the towns or villages themselves, however much the headmasters liked to have their staff at hand. In practical terms it meant I had to take the six o'clock train to school and be back at home in the middle of the afternoon. My belated humble lunch was always enjoyed, shared with our neighbours' dog, a cute little beige mongrel who always sat on our doorstep, knowing exactly the time I would return. Then followed the routine of 4–6 hours practising at the piano; this was needed if I was to succeed at the music examination to be taken as an external student at the Brno conservatoire.

This way of life was almost idyllic compared with what followed some time after the end of November 1944. I was sent to teach in a small town in the mountainous area – a beautiful place with that roomy secondary modern school, but difficult to get to by public transport. To own a car was a great exception, but in war time private cars were confiscated anyway. My usual commuter train terminated half-way, the other half of the journey had to be taken by coach, if only it would deliver me in time for school, before 8 a.m. During the war time the coach went up once a day, in the middle of the morning, and back in the middle of the afternoon. What to do? Look for accommodation – which was difficult and did not really suit me? The date of my music examination was approaching rapidly; moving my piano was impossible and anyway, who would accommodate me with such an encumbrance?

My rations of cigarettes (non-smokers had them, too) came in useful as a reward (or a bribe?) to a couple of forest workers who gave me a lift in their lorry from the railway station to my school, but, oh, the anxiety every day lest I come late to school! Snow lay everywhere, roads remained uncleared . . . Then, what I feared, happened. My train was greatly delayed by transports of Nazi soldiers and the forest workers could not wait for me. In any case, all civilians intending to continue their journey later by coach were ordered to walk to a crossroad, as if to board the vehicle there.

Instead, a huge machine gun stood there, turned against us. No, they did not shoot us – they just left us standing in the snow for a couple of hours until the coach arrived. There was nothing else to do but to board it with the crowd (would the machine gun operate if we tried to disperse?). By this time the teaching hours would be almost over given the time I was likely to arrive. The coach moved slowly, labouring in the snow drifts, even stopping occasionally – my chance to get out and return home?!

Alas! Nobody knew then that the Germans had come to raid the mountains, to catch the partisans, parachutists or scouts, the keen Czech saboteurs hiding there, and that the whole area was encircled. There were soldiers on both sides of the road and no other people to be seen far and wide. Every few yards I had to respond to a "Halt!" and explain what I was doing there; it took me well over an hour to cover the distance of about a mile, to reach the headquarters where I was sent. More explanation and fear – but, they let me go! I came home very late that day, but my ordeal proved to have been worth it: the whole area was closed for a full three weeks – not a soul could slip through, not even the indispensable miners were allowed to go to their work beyond these boundaries.

The school inspector understood well why I could not get to my school – we had to wait and see. Back at my piano, the anxiety concerning the raid remained with me: the husband of my close friend, an officer of the now disbanded Czech army, was among the hunted. Thank heaven, they did not catch him; he returned safely home at the end of the war, but it was a long time before we heard this good news.

I took my music examination at the beginning of January 1945 when it was pretty clear that the end of the war was within sight. My aunt who put me up those few nights during the examination lived fairly near to the conservatoire and I thought that I knew the way there quite well. The street was gently sloping downwards, as I remembered, and the building itself was on the left. The examinees were allowed to come there the night before, to try the instrument on which they were to perform. Fine – never mind the blackout! Yes, the street was sloping downwards, but suddenly it went up, just near where I expected the conservatoire to be. It was pitch-dark – had I lost the way? All of a sudden I bumped into a large building. Then I realized that the neighbouring house to the conservatoire was earlier hit by a bomb, its rubble had created "a mountain" which covered the entrance to the conservatoire. Ascending this mountain I could enter, like the rest of us, to the conservatoire through the window on the first floor.

Towards the end of April 1945 we could already hear the rattling of the machine guns of the Russian army approaching from the east. Our family house, situated in an East-Moravian town, had an almost strategic position on the corner of the main thoroughfare and an insignificant side-road; soon enough we spotted two German scouts hiding behind our lilac hedge, anxiously watching the main road. The retreat of their army seemed inevitable and yet, would they, perhaps, plunder and take revenge on the civilians before they surrendered? Only a few days earlier they had dragged away the remaining handful of Jewish members who had been allowed to stay up to now with their gentile spouses; what could one expect at this critical hour?

The two scouts came to our door, asking politely if they could borrow our doormat to sit on – a small price to pacify them. We sighed with relief. The noise of the bullets eased for a while, only to be renewed with increased vigour. Just then the two scouts knocked at our door again. No, they did not come to kill us; they just returned the doormat, thanked us and disappeared quickly. Another sigh of relief – and one more when the Jewish wife of our neighbour returned home: the captors had no time to exterminate them when their own skin was at stake!

Yet, they did not seem to be willing to surrender. The town was besieged for three days, the two armies changing hands over it more than once. Several new graves in our cemetery and the bullet-marked façade of our house testified to what was happening while we were sheltering in our cellars and basements. These not very attractive places provided not only shelters for ourselves, but also for the blacklisted books from our libraries, as well as other precious commodities kept specially for the celebration of the end of the war, like preserves, bottled meat and, above all, small national flags to wave welcome to the liberating Russian army. When could they be safely taken out, we wondered.

Sancta simplicitas! How could we think that our flags would impress the hardened front-line soldiers, perhaps convicted criminals among them? They invaded our houses, ate our bottled sausages and apricots, spat and cursed when our bottles yielded only paraffin and vinegar, and threatened to kill us in their disbelief that no alcohol was in the house. Had they ever heard the word "teeto-taller"? Luckily, our watches and similar valuables were well hidden, but our maid had to watch helplessly as her bicycle was dragged away after she was beaten up, because she could not repair the punctured tyre.

These privileged first-line soldiers did not even bother to salute their middle-aged colonel when he appeared on the scene: they remained seated comfortably, one leg stretched to the east, the other to the west, one greasy hand pushing a piece of sausage into the mouth, after which the same greasy hand fished for apricots in the other bottle. Soon enough, the colonel's young girlfriend (surely, she was hardly eighteen?) presented herself in my best, silk dress which I had failed to hide away in time. Perhaps I should not have begrudged it to her as she may have saved the three of us – mother, the maid and myself – from being raped, as several women in our town experienced; our elderly neighbour only just managed to save his daughter and daughter-in-law by hiding them carefully in the middle of his compost heap.

The dark-skinned, pock-marked and very short colonel decided that the best room in our house, my late father's study, should be his and his girlfriend's bedroom. Frequent comings and goings changed our quiet home into a "house of passage"; our treasured, polished oak parquet floors moaned under the hobnailed boots of our "liberators". The siege being over, we could leave the cellars, but only the bravest dared to go out to the streets to see what was happening. The fame of the Russians' greed for watches preceded their actual "visits" to our houses, so that we could hide at least some, but, in spite of that, some soldiers were seen with their arms covered with watches, enjoying their ticking. When the watches needed winding, they just considered them useless and threw them to the river. Pubs had no drinks to sell, but the soldiers always seem to have found enough to get properly drunk; arguments arose among them, shots were heard – and new graves appeared in our cemetery. What value human life if there are so many of them?

We lost our radio, too, but some neighbours managed to save theirs until the first wave was over. In the middle of the turmoil in our town the news about a dreadful massacre in Prague was announced: the Czechs wished to liberate their capital themselves and reckoned that, if need be, Patton's army, now in Pilsen, was bound to reach Prague quickly enough to help drive the German occupants to their ultimate surrender. Uninformed about the details of the Yalta agreement, the Prague patriots rose far too early: Patton's army was not allowed to move beyond Pilsen and the Russians had some 200 miles to fight their way to Prague. When I came to the capital about a month later I could see the devastation of the buildings, including the shattered, scorched old Town Hall, as well as the streets strewn with little shrines, marking places where young defenders of Prague died.

The first taste of the renewed liberty had a bitter tang, but it had to be overcome, especially when the true end of the war could really be celebrated. After six years in the Nazi cage we were free again! Resentment against the Western army could hardly be avoided, even if they acted correctly according to the Allies' agreement; the Russians were greeted as the true liberators. If only we had known *how fatal* the Yalta agreement was for us! And those partisans hiding in the forests and carrying out acts of sabotage during the war: their families were stranded then, left to our help and good will. How little we suspected that many of them were organized communists worming their way through into the system already then! Or: idealists? How much did *they* know about the true face of communism? They did good anti-Nazi work during the war. Who were they in the melting pot? The euphoria over the liberation seems to have cast a veil in our minds over the beastly behaviour of the first Russian army. Their childish ways combined as they were with the clumsiness of the Russian bear made us even laugh in retrospect; jokes about them flourished. Yet, they had defeated our greatest enemy, the Nazis. Were they communists? What did Communism stand for? The West had let us down once again (had it?), people thought, scantily informed as we were. In this spirit many Czechs gave their votes to the communists at the ill-fated first free election in 1946. Our liberators – the uniformed men with bunches of flowers, kissing and hugging our babies in the streets – could they do any harm to us? Yes, they could. On 21 August 1968 the liberators turned up as occupants.

A month after the armistice in 1945, Czech universities were re-opened. The first three months, June–September, were regarded as the first "semester", so that our lost time could be curtailed at least a little. It seemed to me that my mother never seriously saw me as a university student, especially as now I was a well-qualified teacher. Yet, she yielded to my plea to join three of my former classmates, all male, to enrol in Prague immediately. Imagine the six-year accumulation of students who had to postpone their studies! The large lecture theatre of the Faculty of Philosophy was packed; not only all the seats were filled, but also all steps, window sills and the rostrum round the lecturer who could not move one pace. Our enthusiasm was great, but not all of us could stand the pressure: the gap for those who had left school 4–5 years before was too great to get back to any effective study; their "mortality" was considerable. Hardly any textbooks were available and we had to rely on the lecture material, but the greatest worry was accommodation. I was lucky to have a married brother living in Prague. After his marriage in 1942, in spite of the great shortages, he managed to find a small flat, adequate for two; now the first baby was there, too, but a bed could be erected for me in their sizeable kitchen for the time being. Student hostels, far too few for the crowds, were filled instantly, so my three colleagues slept a few nights in railway stations or parks, until a passer-by addressed them and took pity on them. No, he had no spare rooms, but they could have a roof overhead if they slept in the entrance hall – which the students gratefully accepted as an improved emergency measure.

The fatal February 1948 caught me living in a flat belonging to a communist family of three. My room had twin beds so that my mother could stay with me for even longer periods, which she preferred to being left alone in our Moravian home, after our maid had left to get married. I was too busy with my studies to get involved in anything else, least of all in politics. How could one expect that a communist *putsch* might be imminent? On that fatal day, 25 February, my landlady barged into our room at 6 a.m., shouting: "Heavens above! The whole town is in the streets and you still in bed!" Yes, she was a truly fiery communist, berating anyone who was only lukewarm, like her husband, or cool, like my mother and myself. Obviously, it would be dangerous to stay in this flat for much longer . . .

The new régime still claimed to be democratic, but what kind of democracy is it if a straitjacket is imposed almost immediately? The new illegal exodus of people belonging to the opposite political camp soon began, as they tried to escape persecution. The frontiers were closed and watched. Barriers, barbed wire, watch towers were gradually installed to prevent their escape. Yet, many, especially intellectuals, managed to get through. Normal travel abroad had to stop because many people would just choose to stay abroad as exiles; occasional offers of small grants from Western universities remained unused, as nobody could be trusted to return to the communist "paradise".

Horrible political purges took place a few months before my final first-degree examination. In addition, a new compulsory test – in Marxism – had to be passed before anyone could be admitted to the finals. How did I pass? For me, there was no harm in learning anything; I thought that it may be just as well to know my enemy. A lot depended on the examiner. Mine was still a student, brought to power by his staunch support of the party. Obviously, he liked my blue eyes. He stared, he examined; he did not interrogate. I was lucky!

Soon after I started working on my Ph.D. dissertation on George Eliot. My favourite supervisor, Professor O.Vočadlo, the best English scholar on the staff and a staunch liberal, was dismissed from his post as politically undesirable. Kindly paternal, he allowed me to see him unofficially in his home every now and then, not only to be advised, but he also lent me precious books on the subject, as the library could now order only politically "safe" publications. How could George Eliot fit into the "socialist" context? When eventually my dissertation was almost finished, I plucked up courage to contact my new supervisor. This unsmiling, often cynical man had no appeal for me – there was no parallel line in our ways of thinking. Obviously, he was ready to conform with the new ideology, although I suspected that in his heart of hearts he was not nearly so convinced and could only follow the slippery path of pretence. "What? You have been writing on George Eliot? Such a bourgeois author?" he said. This was not very encouraging, but he did not seem malicious as I feared he could be. Seeing the advanced stage of the thesis he conceded that he would have a look at it in due course.

Oh dear, how could one satisfy him? How to interpret George Eliot as a socialist writer? Would Felix Holt's radicalism be acceptable? What about highlighting Adam Bede, the menial worker? Even Silas Marner might qualify in this category? The beautiful *Middlemarch* would never stand a chance in this messing about . . . No, I was not going to sell my soul. I could honestly praise Adam Bede because I admired his reliability and integrity – that would have to do. And it did, although the peevish expression of the examiner, as if the man suffered some injury, was not encouraging. "Actually, there *is* something in it; I have accepted it," he retorted, dismissing me curtly.

With this hurdle over, one more was in store for me before I could graduate fully, the rigorous oral examinations in the main subjects, three hours in succession with three different examiners, and, on another day, one hour in philosophy. Philosophy? Only materialist philosophers were represented on the syllabus; there was no room for the idealists in this "democratic" ideology. The time appointed on the day for the three main subjects was between 8 and 11 a.m. All went well the first two hours, discussing English language in the first and comparing great Russian novels with English ones in the second; very good results in both guaranteed the final "victory", whatever might happen in the third. Encouraged and joyful, I was almost looking forward to the last stage where I should be examined in detail on the nineteenth-century English novel, my favourite subject. Perhaps on this last occasion, the tense, unsatisfactory relationship with this examiner might be improved? But where was he? Ten o'clock passed and there was no sign of him in his study. My two first examiners were still there to see the final result; they phoned, became agitated, anxious and angry. Of course, we would have to start all over again with the three on another day ... No, wait, we shall find him, they tried to pacify me.

He came at 4 o'clock p.m. Exhausted by tension and hunger I was not in the best condition for a duel with this disgruntled-looking man who, it seemed, had forgotten all about me and my vital examination. He did not prepare his questions and, as the English novel was not his specialist field, it was completely ignored. Metaphysical poets, Shakespeare, Marlowe, American literature had to be dug up from the depths of my memory – it was a real shock. For a full hour, there he was, watching me, the odious object who prevented him from doing what he really wanted to and whose presence reminded him of his weak spot, the nineteenth-century English "bourgeois" novelists whom he tried to avoid.

But everything in this world has its end, even if the contrary is sometimes felt. My mother who was expecting me for lunch at noon, met me in tears, worried lest a bad accident had delayed me. Relieved that all was well, her tears brightened into joy.

Now I could resume my neglected general reading as well as my social life, such as was possible among fellow students. Some undergraduates had left Prague after the purges, to take less satisfactory jobs than they hoped to get if they were allowed to finish their studies. A few disappeared without trace, presumably escaped abroad; my two uncles who spent the war in Britain were there again now, having left in time. My brother was dismissed from his post in the Ministry of Culture a few days after the *putsch* and held now a humble position elsewhere, sheltered as much as possible from the eagle eye of the régime. There were no party members in my family. I was branded! What future for me? The monster trials and executions of Rudolf Slánský, a former communist, and Dr. Milada Horáková, a prominent member of the previous opposition (by now, there was *no* effective opposition) were to serve as a warning. What future was for me?

In the earlier years of the communist régime the idea of an exile hardly entered my head. How could I leave my mother? My brother, aunts, cousins, friends? In 1952, escape seemed almost impossible as the electrified barriers surrounded the whole country, watch towers illuminated the ground far and wide, guard dogs could sniff you. The methods of escape for those who were still getting over every now and then became more and more ingenious, as the risk of being caught increased. The frontier guards were now free to shoot without warning. No, this was not for me, I thought, I have to resign myself to the dreary life in the totalitarian state.

One day in June, around lunch time, one of my student friends, Tom, appeared unexpectedly at my door. "If you want to go, be ready at the main railway station at 4 p.m. Just light clothing, but don't forget your gum boots!, personal documents, not much else – it's going to be a long walk. OK?" This came as a thunderbolt. If I had had more time to think, I rather doubt that I would have done it.

Adversity

Chapter II

"Over the hills" to Austria
Vienna
first impressions and shocks
screening in the British zone of Vienna

The coach reached its terminus in a small village at half-past six in the evening. It was cloudy, but there was still too much daylight to start towards the frontier. The main road was watched, so we had to take a path across the fields. This led us, for about half-an-hour, to our destination, a small cottage in the next village where the third and most important member of the party was already waiting. It could not possibly be done without him, because he knew the way. His parents lived near the frontier in south Moravia and he knew the district well. Every vacation during the last few years when he came home from the university town, he used to go out for walks to observe the barriers and guards at the frontier, and to learn about their movements. At last he was confident that the crossing would be safe. He agreed to take two more people with him, but was rather upset when Tom brought a girl. "Impossible. We cannot go. She might not be strong enough for the long journey and would ruin everything."

He knew that three lives were at stake, if now, in 1952, the guards were allowed to shoot without warning. On the other hand, there was a serious risk in leaving me behind: I might be stopped and questioned on my way back and then his family would be in danger. It could not be helped, there was nothing for it but to take me along.

Rain fell as the night approached. The three of us put on our gumboots and started off. We crossed the back garden, climbed over the fence and then disappeared among the heavy crops of a large cornfield. We had to walk fast, as fast as the wet corn allowed us; in five minutes we were soaked through up to our waists. Who would care in such a situation? When the rain stopped it was pitch dark; our guide knew why he insisted on going on a moonless night. There were more cornfields to cross: how angry would the farmer be finding his crop flattened by intruders! We had to find a shorter way; the narrow, gradually overgrowing path was still too public for escapees, even though, apart from the guards, no human being would normally dare to use it.

The countryside was absolutely flat and the few lights on the horizon seemed to be miles and miles away. Yes, they were the destination – the Austrian side. But the distance! Is it really possible to walk that far during one night? Although it was early summer, the damp grass was withered and only a few patches of a neglected field, ruins of a cottage and a solitary wayside cross reminded us that people lived here not so long ago. There was no time or light enough to examine in detail the expression on Christ's martyred face on this monument, but its very presence had a strange effect on me: abandoned physically, as if He were abandoned spiritually, too, in a world where you were kept prisoner in your own country.

A strip of land quite a few miles wide before the frontier was absolutely lifeless; it was the "neutral" zone. Signposts reminded us of the fact, but our guide tried to avoid them; to our minds it was better to be ignorant of the line where the greatest danger began. There was an eerie silence and nobody had to be warned not to talk; the fear and expectation of the future made us watchful.

After some three-hours' walk suddenly we heard a bark about three hundred yards behind us. If it is the guards, we were lost. No? I felt a shudder go down my spine but our leader kept cool. He knew that this could be expected. He took us by the hand, hurried us up and pacified us by remarking casually that it was only a fox. There was no house near where a dog could be kept and he could not afford to break our courage by admitting the truth. The barking was not repeated and the expected shooting did not take place; obviously, there was already a considerable distance between us and the guards.

Unexpectedly, after the next hour's walk, another hazard had to be overcome, namely, a river. There was no time to take off the boots; fortunately, the river was only about three feet deep and could be waded across fairly quickly. The sound of the disturbed water was just as terrifying as the silence around. Then came the moment of the greatest anxiety. The river was crossed without a hitch, but the gumboots, full of water, made a lot of noise and had to be taken off to be emptied. What an incredibly difficult task! They stuck to the wet feet like leeches; precious minutes were lost while we struggled with the boots, first one's own, then helping each other – I do not know which was the more successful in the end, but, at last, it was done! Still, the guide got nervous as more time was lost than he reckoned and his plan was slightly thwarted. A little copse of trees offered a hideout; back on the horizon it was becoming slightly lighter, but among the trees it was still so dark that we had to hold each other by hand in order to keep together.

All of a sudden, the leader gasped: "Stop! Don't move!" This was to prevent even the slightest noise. The river was behind us and, on the bridge, about twenty-five yards away from our hideout, the silhouettes of two guards and a dog were looming against the horizon. Had they heard? Had they not? Not a word was said, of course, but, secretly, we were counting how many more minutes we could be spared, as, no doubt, we were going to be shot. Did they suspect – or not? No, they did not, nor was there any danger of the breeze betraying our presence to the dog – the wind was blowing in the opposite direction. Thank heaven!

The twenty minutes of motionless standing were almost unbearable; they seemed like two hours. At last, the silhouettes of the guards, now returning, appeared on the bridge again. Soon they were gone and we could continue our journey. It seemed endless even for such good walkers as we were. The worst two-thirds were over, but there was no sign of the actual frontier yet. We had to speed up, as the delay was considerable and the danger not yet over. How many more miles? Heaven only knew – and who cared? The die was cast and there was no retreat. We walked on in the dark night.

At last the first signs of dawn appeared on the horizon and the darkness and the silence became less oppressive. The shape of some trees, as if along a lane, appeared in the distance. When we reached them, it was already daylight. The air was clean and fresh, perhaps a bit cold to make us feel comfortable in our wet clothes, but we walked briskly, as the Austrian border was now near. Was it really the frontier? A simple, inconspicuous milestone informed us that here the Austrian territory started. Just one more jump over the ditch and the worst was over.

Oh, no, we were still not fully out of danger. There was no

neutral zone in Austria as on the other side of the Iron Curtain, but the four armies of occupation were still in Austria and this particular zone was occupied by the Russians. That is why the Iron Curtain still had a few loopholes in this section: the refugees could be caught on the other side of the border just the same. But at least we could presume that the Austrian guards would not shoot without warning. It appeared as if the Austrians firmly believed in the impenetrability of the Iron Curtain as the frontier did not seem to be guarded, or, at least, not much. Fortunately, the guide knew all the paths and short cuts; although the way to Vienna from the frontier was longer than the walk in the night, everything seemed simpler and straightforward.

What a relief to get safely to the American zone in Vienna! I was rewarded by a pat on the shoulder for having caused no trouble on the journey; in fact, I was quite useful when I produced an address of people who might offer us the very first refuge. I had never met them, but knew that they were old friends of my aunt. When we arrived at the address, the people looked rather doubtful at the sight of three soaked and battered figures, but my aunt's name worked like magic. Refuge was offered readily without much enquiring; the good people weren't even surprised that we could sleep non-stop for the rest of the day. They helped us to clean and iron out our clothes, so that we could appear in the street like normal people, but they were not able to advise us further about how to seek asylum; they had never had this experience before.

What could be done? We had no idea what new refugees should expect. When we lived on the other side of the Iron Curtain, information had not been available as, in many respects, the border was almost hermetically sealed from the rest of the world. We only knew what we wished to do: in order to be useful to our suffering country, we should remind people in the West of its predicament as much as possible. Our guide, who had relatives in America, wanted to go there and finish his studies. Tom and I wished to go to Britain, where, we thought, democracy would be most welcome for a quiet, non-political way of life. The communist régime never allowed us to travel abroad and we had no chance to practise the English language which we studied at the university; also, the possibilities of further study and research were very limited. But, in the first place, it was freedom for which, we thought, it was worth risking our lives. The atmosphere in the communist country was too suffocating and dangerous for young, keen people who believed that one can work quietly, away from all political life. During the German occupation, one could be left alone as long as one was not an outspoken liberal and did not interfere with the Nazis; this was not so in the communist régime who insisted that those who did not go with them must be against them. Consequently, such a person was suspected, pestered by agents and eventually persecuted.

Those numerous people who left the country for the other side of the Iron Curtain were rarely heard of afterwards. Once there were some horrible stories in the newspapers about DP (displaced persons) camps. Surely, it cannot be true, we thought, that must be simply communist propaganda! We knew only too well how information was twisted in the communist press. Surely, if one seeks asylum in the West, is it not obvious that one is coming as a friend and admirer? There cannot be so much difficulty for honest people who are ready to work; all that was needed was to go to the British authorities, explain the situation and offer one's services. Then, to get the necessary travel documents and leave Vienna as soon as possible. At least, so we thought, naive and ignorant as we were.

Of course, it turned out to be not so simple. Our trio split the next day: our guide went to the American Embassy while the two of us to the British; in fact, we did not hear from him for a long time until, some four years later, a Christmas card came from him, saying that he finally got to the United States, but that after such a long break he could not cope with his studies and gave them up. By then we knew better; we were no longer so naive and therefore not surprised.

We found the British Embassy in Vienna, but before we could be admitted to the Secretary, we were intercepted by a policeman in British uniform, with a heavy truncheon under his arm. Heavens! Are we criminals and are we being led to jail? Of course, we had crossed the frontier illegally; but so had many other people – are they all imprisoned? It was not exactly a prison where we were taken, although later we learned that some refugees were actually charged by the Austrians and were made to serve short-term sentences.

The seat of the British Foreign Secret Service where we were taken was more like a private house: but it did feel like a prison at first. Isn't it enough to give one's name and profession and tell where one would like to go? Isn't it obvious that, risking as much as one's life, one came as a friend? No, it was not, there were many more questions. Are you interested in what is going on in our country? Certainly, we are very pleased to tell you; everybody should know about the people's suffering and perhaps you could help? No, unfortunately, we don't know much about military objects; we have just finished our studies which, of course, was our only interest. You don't believe us? Yes, of course, it is your job to enquire, but as students of the humanities we really didn't notice much what was happening in the technical fields; actually, please, excuse our ignorance, but we are not quite sure what "jet plane" means . . . Surely, you can't mistrust us – you must see that there is no earthly reason why we shouldn't speak but the truth! However, the feeling of being mistrusted crept into the minds of Tom and me. "These two newcomers must be squeezed as lemons", I overheard as I was approaching the room where I was summoned. The officers certainly tried to be efficient, but it was not very pleasant to be their instruments. For their excuse, only later did we hear that a great number of spies from among the intelligentsia had come from behind the Iron Curtain just then, and caution was necessary.

During the meals and in the breaks when we were not questioned one could talk to the other refugees – about ten altogether – who were in a similar position. Where do you come from? Did you have a difficult crossing? I got over by crossing the widest spot of the Danube; yes, of course, I had done a lot of swimming and practised nearly a year in the local swimming pool to be sure to last out. Naturally, I was exhausted, because there were obstacles such as barbed wire in the river and, in the end, when getting on to the bank, I was attacked by a rat who had bitten through the strap of my waterproof bag, and so I have lost all my documents. Most annoying, most annoying...

Another young man had his arm and shoulder in bandages. "I came out of hospital only a few days ago," he said. "The frontier guard shot at me. I went one Sunday on a pleasure trip by steamer on the Danube and when it reached the nearest point to the frontier I jumped out and swam towards it. Two policemen immediately chased me, but did not catch me in the water; only as I was climbing the steep bank, on top of which was already the frontier, a third policeman shot at me from the boat. The wound was deep, and through the exhaustion and loss of blood, I collapsed right across the frontier line. An Austrian guard who just happened to be on the spot when the shooting occurred, saved my life simply by dragging me to the Austrian side, while one of the prosecutors was just about to seize me by my leg! Blessed Austrians!"

"Well, ehm, blessed Austrians? I don't know," said another refugee. "I had a fairly easy crossing, but when I came to Vienna and asked for asylum at the police station, they put me in a horrible jail! They told me that illegal crossing of the frontier in any circumstances was trespass against the law, and I was to keep quiet and wait for the trial. You see, one doesn't really know who are masters here. The Austrians don't feel defeated, because, on the whole, they didn't altogether like the idea of Hitler's occupation of Austria and being dragged into the war; but the four occupation powers obviously hold a different opinion. It took about a week before I was released from the prison. And, you see, there was no trial – it was the Austrians who had to give in."

Sometimes, an old Austrian who served as a messenger to the officers joined in the conversation. "Just be patient, my children, just be patient. I know, you would like to emigrate and settle down. But you won't be long here. What? Two weeks? Oh, there were people who had to stay here for two months, or even longer. But, surely, that won't happen in your case. You know that you have to get to the British zone first – and that is still quite a way through the Russian zone. You think that you will be flown there? Oh no, that has never been done before – that would be too expensive! Yes, the Americans may do it, but these people here think it less conspicuous if you go by train on your own. By car? Oh no, you don't understand! A car or jeep may easily be stopped and the Russians wouldn't allow you to be removed in front of their very eyes. You see, they are still one of the Allied Powers . . . "

Such was the reality. Law-abiding people like us would have to undergo the nerve-racking experience of crossing the border once more. A nightmare! Fortunately, this was to be only a passing one; there was another nightmare, much worse and much more permanent: what was happening at home? No member of the family knew about the intended escape; if they did, they would be liable to prosecution, because the authorities expected everybody to denounce the traitor – even a member of his own family – who wished to leave the communist paradise. Also, everybody knew how many people had lost their lives when crossing the frontier – how could a mother bear the agony, knowing that her child might be one of the victims?

Tom and I sent cards home, signed by fictional names but recognizable by the family, the very first day in Vienna: a horrible truth for our mothers (Tom's mother was also a widow), but better than uncertainty and anxiety. At least they knew that we were alive!

Of course, the relatives were bound to be questioned, the police would ransack their houses and confiscate our property (such as it was with two impecunious students!) . . . However, neither Tom nor myself had ever been politically active in our home country, so perhaps it wouldn't be so bad in this respect. The shock of sudden separation – perhaps for ever – was much worse, especially for my mother. I was not the only child, but I knew that I was the favourite. I loved my mother dearly and it seemed natural that we should always live together. How would she take the news of my departure? I could easily imagine, although I tried hard not to do so; it did not help now, anyway. But I felt a great anxiety mixed with nostalgia; my heart seemed as if bruised. How could I leave my mother? I didn't know myself how I could have plucked up the courage. The time for making up my mind was so short – and it was a chance which would not repeat itself. Although usually calm, I nearly got into a panic when I was put face to face with this dilemma. Then I was sitting, staring blankly in my student digs. Instead of packing my little knapsack, I started reading the Bible in order to forget about everything else. Oh, no, it's no use thinking back – but the feeling round my heart was inexpressibly tight, then and for a long time afterwards.

The days passed. The refugees lived in a former private house, furnished sparsely in a military fashion, but apart from the lack of privacy there was no reason to complain against material discomfort. But we had no money. It did not occur to us that the devalued currency of our country would be worth anything in the West, and we had left practically everything at the cottage at the frontier. It did not matter very much, really, but it was inconvenient when, for instance, a shoelace snapped. How to find the few pennies to buy a new one? I should never have thought that I might have to walk in the street with the shoe tied by a piece of string which I found in the park. And how glad I was to have it!

After about a fortnight Tom and I were allowed to visit our Viennese friends, and even go for little walks in the streets within the British zone. Looking at the shop windows full of foodstuffs, sweets, fruit, lovely dresses, suits and shoes, we thought that they were for a mere decoration – surely not for sale? Of course, our country used to be well off and just as prosperous as this flourishing Vienna, but now, seven years after the war, the best produce was sent to the Soviet Union and much was wasted by inefficiency and work-shyness.

Vienna! Was this the celebrated gay and carefree city of Strauss, where our grandparents went occasionally to enjoy themselves? Certainly not, or, at least, it did not appear to us as such. The first thing that struck us was something strange, calm, in the atmosphere. Before we left our country, the sense of a possible war in the near future was felt there ever so strongly. There were too many expressions like "fight", "struggle", "weapon", "defeat", "crush", "challenge", in the slogans calling for peace. As if people of small countries did not know this kind of consolation! Wasn't it like that before the First and Second world wars? Sometimes in history wars have brought better life and freedom to our country; perhaps this will be another such occasion, and very soon, too? It could not go on like that; a democratically-minded nation could not bear a tyrannical régime for long, neither could the free world stand by, helplessly watching the insidious spread of communism! The people on the eastern side of the Iron Curtain, being insufficiently informed about what was going on in the politics of the West, could not believe that the free world would not burn their fingers when a few small (or not so small) nations lost their freedom.

There was peace in Vienna. No slogans, no fear in people's eyes, no sign of an approaching war. Thank heaven for that; who would wish for a new war? But, does it mean that our country is doomed to remain in the cage for ever? Does it mean that we shall never be able to return and see our dearest ones? Impossible! However, the seed of doubt was sown in our minds then, even if we resisted it with all our might.

One day, two travelling agents came to the house where the refugees lived, and tried to gain access to the flat. The officers were to be found in another house nearby, and, by the time the old messenger could bring some of them, the two men left, disappearing from our sight quickly so as not to create suspicion. Of course! Communist spies could be everywhere; they knew about the places of secret services in Vienna. Perhaps they came to find out whether Tom and I were there. Who knows?

Later on, more pleasant visitors came. Newspaper and broadcast reporters were keen to get recent authentic news and we thought them very considerate when they gave us some Austrian money. At last, new shoelaces could be bought, and it also meant for us an end of shame when, previously, we had to put the small Czech useless coins as offerings in an Anglican church where we went on Sundays. The congregation was very small and we did not know anybody, but we would have felt even more embarrassed to pass the collection bag by and give nothing. How could we explain? And who would have understood? At least, the little coins clinked . . .

There was enough temptation in Vienna to spend the few shillings we had acquired, but we resisted. Not only because they would not buy much, but they might come in useful later on, when perhaps another shoelace might break.

Chapter III

Through the Russian zone to the British
quarantine camp
the ghost of a Labour Office
anxiety and relief

At last, after about five weeks, our screening proved us to be absolutely harmless idealists and dreamers. We were to be sent to the British zone in Austria; farther west – although it was actually south. One evening, Tom and I and a student called Stan were told that we should be ready at 5 a.m. the next day. Of course, we were unable to shut our eyes all night: are we to be caught now, after we got over the most dangerous hazard, crossing the Iron Curtain? The two boys were instructed about the itinerary and how to proceed so as not to create suspicion. With a slight shiver and feeling of bitterness they accepted the information that there would be no leader, that we would have to rely on ourselves only. In the morning we were provided with food for a day and train tickets.

As soon as we entered the train, we ran across a Russian soldier. Our hearts sank, but there was no need to panic. The soldier was off duty and too sleepy at such an early hour to be concerned about three odd-looking tourists. Yet, there were many more Russian soldiers on the train and it was not easy to find a compartment with civilians only; we seemed to see the Russians everywhere.

At last we managed to find a corner where we hoped we would not be addressed by anybody. We had to keep silent as either the foreign language, or our accent if we spoke German, might make some Austrians curious about us. The hours passed and our train journey ended without a hitch. However, the nervous strain of the past weeks in Vienna, the sleepless night and a new anxiety and uncertainty showed their effects. We felt very tired and hungry, but, of course, we would not dream of taking anything out of our provisions at this stage. We must get to safety first!

But, safety lay still far away. There was a good piece of the hilly countryside to cross, and on foot. The train deposited us, but had we taken the right road? That was the question we had to ask ourselves repeatedly for the next four or five hours. Four or five? Who cared how many; they seemed endless, anyway. The summer was very hot that year and we had to start the walking part of the journey at noon. Somehow, this second crossing of the border, although shorter, was much more strenuous than the first. I caused no trouble on the first and more dangerous occasion, but this time, after a while, I felt giddy and nearly collapsed when we climbed a steep hill. They had to give me a few minutes to recover, but no more than a few minutes; we had to move on.

The way seemed to tally with the description the boys were given, up to a certain fork, where either road might be the right one. This must be somewhere near the frontier between the British and Russian zones, as, after a while, we noticed that we were walking round and coming back to the same spot again and again and that, in fact, some 200 yards away, we could see the uniform of a Russian frontier guard. Obviously, we had not taken the right road, but soon the second road led us to safety. It was late afternoon and the sun was nearly setting when we arrived at the little guard station on the British side of the zone. Yes, they were expecting three refugees, but nobody had arrived to take charge of us and we had to wait. How long? Sorry, the man on duty could not tell.

At last we ate some of our provisions and waited. Heaven knows whether it was tiredness or anxiety we had just suffered, that made us doubt whether we had reached the right spot, whether we had not been, somehow, betrayed. Our former life under the communists, based on hatred, fear and mutual mistrust, taught us a lesson. How can we trust anyone? We knew of people who had paid to be escorted across the Iron Curtain, but instead were led straight to the communist authorities. In Vienna we were not ill-treated, but neither were we cared for as friends; after we had to accept this second crossing made more dangerous than necessary, we could hardly help feeling like squeezed lemons, of no use to anybody any more.

Nothing happened during the next three to four hours. The waiting increased the anxiety and mistrust; our nerves were on edge as we watched intently every movement of the guard as well as the whole surroundings. That was all we could do; we were now in his hands and any action would be neither useful nor wise.

It was very late in the evening when a British officer in a jeep turned up. Yes, he had the same uniform as the officers in Vienna, so perhaps all was well, after all. Anyway, we were so exhausted that really nothing mattered any more. The jeep swallowed us up and we did not care where we were driven. In a state between sleep and wake, we could not tell how long we spent in the jeep, but the journey seemed very long.

Where were we going? Was the old messenger in Vienna right in saying that in the British zone every refugee had to pass through a quarantine? Perhaps so; it did not matter much, because it would be only for two weeks – and, besides, one could get the long-wished-for documents there. Actually, this was quite a pleasant prospect: all three of us were perfectly healthy, so there should not be any complications in this respect, and if we got the necessary documents, we would be able to leave Austria for England.

The old messenger was right. It was a quarantine, but this one looked rather different from what I imagined quarantine quarters would be. It would not matter if it was a camp, but it was highly probable that this one served previously as one of Hitler's concentration or labour camps. Only the high fence of barbed wire was replaced by ordinary wire netting, finished off by only one row of barbed wire. The camp, somewhere south of Graz, consisted of about six barracks, built in a circle, in the centre of which a large hut, divided into a number of very primitive lavatories, dominated the scene. There were hardly any formalities, as it was in the middle of night, when we were handed over to the camp. The men were shown into one of the barracks and I into another, reserved for women.

All the time since I left my country I had not come across a woman refugee and I feared that I might be alone in this uninviting hut. It was a pleasant surprise to find that only one of the seven "beds" was free, just waiting for me. Now I should have the company of my own sex – that was a cheering prospect. They were all asleep and the darkness prevented me from getting a full view of the room.

I did notice, however, that the room had no proper floor and my bed reminded me of something which Robinson Crusoe on a desert island might have been able to put up as a bed, except that he would have had a piece of luxurious fur instead of the rough grey blanket, and dry leaves instead of the lumpy straw in the sack beneath. The bedstead was made of raw, unplaned trunks or branches of spruce; but what did it matter when one was tired?

I stretched myself on the bed fully dressed, not only because I had no nightdress, but mainly because the clothes would smother the effect of the prickly straw. There was very little of the night left and soon beautiful sunshine gave a warm welcome to the three newcomers, to lift their depression at finding themselves in a place as desolate as this. My room-mates were farm workers, mainly from Yugoslavia. That was something new to me: do people leave Yugoslavia, too? Have they not more freedom there than in other communist countries? Perhaps they do, but, obviously, it was still worth leaving.

Unfortunately, and that was an unpleasant discovery for the Yugoslavs, they were not given the status of political refugees and their position in Austria was extremely precarious. They could be sent back any moment! On the other hand, they were much better off materially than the refugees from the "proper" satellite countries, because, and that was something inconceivable for the other refugees, their relations or friends could come over legally and bring them clothes or whatever else they needed. Is it possible that someone might flee one's country for political reasons and his mother could still get a passport for a visit in a Western country? What a queer muddle . . .

However, the Austrians, heaven forgive them, could make some sense out of this. In this way they could get cheap farm labourers who seemed to be in short supply in that area. It did not seem to matter whether the person in question was a farm worker or a professor of philosophy in his country.

The first day in the camp, all the three of us felt very tired. We were given billy cans and joined the queue to get our breakfast which consisted of about half a pint of black malt-and-chicory coffee, sweetened with saccharin, and about half of a small loaf of Austrian brown bread. The more experienced inmates warned us that this was the ration of bread for the whole day and that we should keep some for supper.

This proved to be a wise move, as the evening meal differed from the breakfast only by the absence of bread. The leftovers of the provision, obtained in Vienna, came in very useful, but how would we manage when this ran out? A few of the Yugoslavs had help in this respect from the outside, as mentioned before; others had some money with which a messenger who went down town twice a day, could bring them what they wanted.

This possibility was rather hard on the three of us, as, our future being most uncertain, we were determined to keep the few shillings earned in Vienna in reserve for a rainy day. The stay in this camp was limited to two weeks. This was an agreeable thought because, who would wish to stay longer? We hoped that we might survive on the camp food for that length of time without spending our money on extra food, but even I, for whom food was of no great concern, decided on the ninth day to get two extra rolls so as not to feel quite so hungry.

The breakfast was the same every day and likewise the supper on most days, except that the "coffee" was sometimes replaced by a cup of skimmed milk; lunches consisted of potatoes with cabbage or carrots or another vegetable. On Thursdays there used to be "stew", containing three-quarters of water and one-quarter of potatoes among which, if one was lucky, one or even two mouthfuls of meat might be floating. On Sundays, there was a small slice of beef for everybody – lucky or unlucky!

If one had not discovered gradually that this insufficient food was one of the measures of the highest economy possible, one might have thought that it was one of the means of testing the health and endurance of the consumers. One could also think its aim was to coarsen one's palate: the scene on Fridays, with the buxom, plump cook, serving with the look of greatest pride the horrid *polenta* out of a huge couldron, was unforgettable and amusing, even if the whole action seemed to have some punitive tang. It would not matter so much that the porridgy stuff was boiled in water instead of milk (this was replaced by a few spoonfuls of skimmed milk on top of each helping); one could even overlook the fact that there was no sugar on or in it, but one could hardly imagine that the complete absence of salt in this dish would help the Austrian economy a great deal.

Austrian or British? It was difficult to say for certain in whose hands the responsibility lay. The question "who is master here" came up again: the camp was in the British zone and the British, as it seemed, expected Austria to pay her war debt; the Austrians, on the other hand, did not feel guilty and resented being put on a level with the Germans who caused the impoverishment of their country. Grudgingly they took the material responsibility over the camp because they had to, but, being poor themselves, they would gladly apply what actually Hitler had taught them, namely, the highest degree of material economy. The British then took responsibility for the political leadership of the camp. Rightly or wrongly, it looked as if two cooks had spoiled the broth which the refugees were tasting.

The camp was run by a typical, broad and jovial Austrian who might have previously been an army officer; he was called *Herr Direktor*, which title he assumed with a complacent smile, just as other directors from the old Austro-Hungarian Empire would do, no matter whether they "directed" a large bank in Vienna or a small, one-form primary school in a tiny Alpine village. His respect for rank seemed to indicate his army past; fortunately, apart from his own directorial title, he respected other people's titles equally highly – just as one would expect from a typical, polite Austrian. This fact proved to be a blessing for me, as it gave me thirteen fairly good nights of rest instead of sleepless ones. It happened simply that just the first night all the bugs in the camp, or at least in that particular barrack, made a great campaign to attack this newcomer with, obviously, the sweetest blood of all the seven female inmates. No one else suffered at all, but I was quite ill as my body was covered with bug bites all over. Heaven knows whether *Herr Direktor* would have cared if it had happened to someone else, but I was *Frau Doktor* for him and, consequently, the barrack was disinfected. When eventually I recovered, I found it rather amusing that for the first time my academic title came in useful. The whole event, though, I must confess, made me anxious. By now, I had no illusions about our being treated with great consideration; would this special attraction I had for bugs be held against my good state of health? If so, what would happen? Should I be sent to another quarantine camp and thus be separated from my companions? The couple of days while the bug bites were healing and my temperature was getting back to normal were not very cheerful.

During the two weeks in the quarantine the refugees were not allowed to leave the place, but they were expected to do light work there, such as cleaning and keeping the barracks and their surroundings tidy. They had to clean and scrub the wooden floors (how strange to see proper floor again!) in the adjoining hospital and in an old people's home. The home was not part of the camp – at least, not any longer. It belonged to a group of very similar primitive barracks, inhabited by German-speaking immigrants, mainly from Transylvania, whom Hitler had brought *"heim ins Reich"* (back home). Was it possible that these barracks were to be their home for so many years after the war, as an exchange for their comfortable Transylvanian homes where they had to leave most of their property? It was obvious that the inhabitants of these barracks did their best to make them look as pleasant as possible: the sweet peas, climbing on the walls were almost touching. Altogether, the place was most depressing, especially the "hospital", or rather a hut of sick-rooms, which gave an impression of desolation. Seeing all that, one forgot that one was hungry; this hunger, one could hope, was only temporary, but the misery of these poor people looked permanent.

It was rather strange that people in a quarantine were not allowed to leave the camp for a minute and yet could go to scrub the floors in these sick-rooms outside it; was it a test of the refugees' susceptibility to infection? There were germs in abundance, but, somehow, we managed to survive the fortnight unharmed, in spite of the insufficient nourishment and other discomforts and hazards of the camp. It was another favour to me from the *Herr Direktor* that I was sent to scrub the floor only once; instead, and as a great favour, I was to dust and tidy up his office every morning. It was not a hard work and it made the time pass quickly. *Herr Direktor* spoke to me in his quiet, sympathetic way – he was a kind man, really – and sometimes a hint escaped his mouth involuntarily, a hint which helped to construct the picture in my mind of the future of my two compatriots and myself. We were determined to stick together for as long as possible.

The words "Labour Office" had a bitter taste since the time of war, when all the population of the countries occupied by Hitler had so many unpleasant recollections of it. So many people – and the three of us were among them – had to leave their jobs during the war and work in ammunition factories for ridiculously low wages as unskilled labourers! The words "Labour Office" escaped *Herr Direktor's* mouth, but the ghost was not a factory there, but a farm. No, this was not possible, we thought; the British officers knew that Tom and I wished to emigrate to Britain; surely, they would push our case. It should be fairly easy, we thought, after we had been given personal documents.

The British officers, who had their headquarters somewhere in the county town, did not spend much time in the camp; we hardly knew them by sight. They came usually for a couple of hours after lunch, mainly to screen the Yugoslav refugees for whom the camp was the very first refuge. They also interviewed the three of us, made notes of our personal data and had us photographed for the document to be issued to us before we left the camp.

Almost invariably one of the officers came also after supper to collect a beautiful young Italian lady and her *bambino*, and to take them somewhere in a jeep. To leave the camp was forbidden; obviously, this lady was a privileged person in the camp, although, it seemed, her privilege was of quite a different nature from mine. For the camp inmates she was a riddle. She slept alone in one of the barracks – as long as she slept in the camp at all – and not in the same block as the other women; but that might have been, we concluded, because of her child – a sweet little girl of about two. But: why was she here? There were no political reasons for escape from Italy and the less so for a creature who looked so utterly "non-political". She must have felt lonely among the female camp inmates as they could not speak Italian and she could not speak anything but her mother tongue. After a few days, however, a new woman refugee arrived at the camp who could talk to her a little. The beautiful Italian confided to her that she left her husband whom she wished to divorce, and that she was very grateful to the British officers who had allowed her to stay and looked after her so well.

Speaking about privileged persons in the camp perhaps I should mention another young woman, from Yugoslavia, whose privilege was yet of another kind. I liked her very much and we could have become real friends if it weren't for the short time we lived near to each other. She was a trained tailoress and could iron men's trousers most beautifully; consequently she was relieved from the daily duties to do a special and more important job – ironing *Herr Direktor's* trousers. He supplied her with at least two pairs every day, making the best of this unique bargain opportunity either for himself or his friends. The satisfaction was mutual: the woman was proud of the praise of *Herr Direktor* (who looked like a tailor's dummy and very pleased with himself, too), and our respect towards him was the greater when we saw what an incredible amount of clothes he could produce for ironing.

Apart from the general and individual duties, there was not much to do in the camp. We had enough time to look through the wire fence at the ripening corn of the field surrounding the camp on one side, and even farther in the distance, dreaming about the homes we had left, or about the white cliffs of Dover which we longed so much to see and which seemed more and more remote from us.

Sometimes a doctor would come who, for some reason, was mainly interested in the inmates' throats and teeth. Occasionally, radio and newspaper reporters found their way to the camp. Their visits proved to be very profitable for both parties concerned. They got the information they wanted and we, who had not yet any clear idea about the routine of treatment of the refugee problem in Austria, profited even more from their account of what we could expect. We were shocked to have the fact confirmed that, after leaving the camp, we would be handed over to the Labour Office. Then we would be sent individually to farmers who might need us. Couldn't one get something else? "Oh, no, don't be too optimistic. There is great unemployment in Austria already and farm work is the only work available. Even these vacancies, no doubt, will be filled before long if the refugees continue to come from behind the Iron Curtain."

Betrayed again? Betrayed by those whom we considered friends and protectors? The feeling was more bitter than when we were informed in Vienna that we would have to cross the frontier of the Russian zone without a guide. The lemons had been squeezed and were not needed any longer.

The farm work itself would not, actually, matter so much, if it were for a limited period; after all, students in communist countries had to do the same for part of each vacation. But here, it could have been made permanent, as we might be absorbed among the Austrians and, through sheer lack of communication fail to obtain information about possible ways to emigrate. How naive we were with respect to our studying abroad!

Our minds were now in a turmoil. As Tom and I had degrees in English, we knew the British character from reading and through a few personal acquaintances; the English seemed so very kind, so human and sensible! Just the right people among whom we wished to live and for whom to work – but how did our recent experience compare with our old ideas? Why can't we be told, explained and warned straight away? We did not know then that the British at home and the British abroad might be two different types of people; or, perhaps there were special regulations for occupation armies –

Russian or English or American. We did not know, nor did we understand.

No use to moan. Dreamers and trusting ninnies have to pay for the lessons life gives them from time to time; perhaps we would be hardened against the next blow.

The day of release from the camp approached. The three of us used all our free time for preparation of this great event. Our spare sets of underwear had to be washed, because heaven knows when there might be the next chance to do so. The washrooms in this camp had a great advantage compared with the other camp we went through later on, namely, the division of the hut into a number of small rooms. This was for us a proof of British respect for privacy, even if the rooms had no bolts. If they had, they would really have served a useful purpose rather than mere decoration (as we found later in some private English houses). But, never mind, it was fun as we practised patience by standing guard, preventing the others from entering any cubicle at an inconvenient moment. The water was only cold, but the summer was so beautifully warm that even the most spoilt British or American holidaymakers would have put up with it.

It is surprising what one can do when faced with necessity. Having my hair cut by one of the boys was not so difficult as my having to cut theirs. The whole camp helped and advised, which only made me more nervous; it took me a very long time, but the young men looked fairly normal after the treatment. Needless to say, the scissors were borrowed from one of the Yugoslavs; such luxury was beyond our reach then and for long afterwards.

All the three of us were looking forward to leaving the camp, in spite of the new anxiety which clouded over our expectations. Since the Labour Office was responsible for making sure that no tramps or vagabonds were wandering in Austria, all refugees' documents had to be stamped from this office; otherwise the people would lose their right to be on the Austrian soil. How could we obtain it without being sent to a farm? This was our anxiety. From the discussions with the reporters we concluded that one could be set free from this obligation if one had enough money for one's upkeep, so as not to be a burden for the Austrians. As this did not describe our situation, the only possibility was to pretend that it was so, and hope for the best. An awful thought! None of us was an expert liar; what if we were asked to show how much money we had? That would be dreadful – and the anger of the official could have the most awkward consequences. But there did not seem to be any other alternative and we consoled ourselves with the extenuating circumstance that we had an honest intention to avoid bothering the Austrians; after all, we thought, if everybody in our country had spoken the absolute truth to Hitler's emissaries during the war, most of the nation would have been gassed years ago. We felt trapped. Could a pretence save us?

On the morning of the celebrated day of release from the camp the three of us and some other refugees who had completed their fortnight in quarantine were given our personal documents. By now we took it for granted that these would not be passports for England; however, we were surprised that the documents were not even in English, but in German. Obviously, the British considered that they had done their duty both towards their own country and the refugees, and were no longer interested. The documents contained fingerprints and photographs of the holders; needless to say that we looked on the documents like prisoners bleached out by a long stay in prison and dazzled by daylight when released. They also contained the clause that, subject to approval by the Labour Office, the holder was entitled to live in Austrian territory for six months. Of course, there was the holder's name, but also a note that his/her identity was not officially confirmed! How strange it was to read that one was not sure who one was.

No guide was needed to accompany us to the Labour Office. It was easy to find and there was no danger that anyone might fail to report there. Without the magic stamp from the office one could be sent back to where one came from. And what could follow? A few years in prison, inferior employment and a continual watch over the person in question.

The Yugoslavs went in first. They returned duly with the stamp and address of the prospective farm where they were to go. We went in. The official looked very stern. He was surprised that anyone should ask for a non-routine treatment and became sterner still. No, no, that's the regulation and he cannot break it. "You are University graduates, aren't you? I see. But, of course, that does not really change the situation."

We had all sorts of answers ready. The official listened, asked further questions, but interrupted the discussion by frequent denials of our request. "You say you have money to look after yourselves?"

No, not even that would do. "Regulations are regulations." We tried to prolong the conversation – perhaps not everything was lost.

The discussion took another direction. "What were you doing during the war? Oh, so, *Totaleinsatz* . . . (complete action). Which place was it? Oh . . . " The official paused and looked rather upset. Then he stamped the three documents, exempting their owners from the farm duty. "That's where my son fell in the war. He would be your age now . . . " Surprise, sympathy, gratitude and joy – all these emotions were mixed together as we left the official's room. We disappeared from the area of the Labour Office with a tremendous speed. Free at last!

Chapter IV

*From the British zone to the American
screening
life in a DP camp*

We got on to the train and counted how much money we had left after having paid for the tickets. Yes, it would do for a modest meal, but we should make do with just a few rolls, so we could still have a few shillings in reserve.

It was good to be on the train. Unfortunately, we were not travelling to England, even if the train carried us westward. That country seemed to us more distant now than ever. Stan decided to try for America; but Tom and I still obstinately clung to the idea of Britain, although we were absolutely in the dark about how to achieve this. Obviously, we were not wanted and now, going to the American zone, which might be taken as a sign of disloyalty, would spoil our chances still more. Yet, there was no other alternative, or, at least, we did not know of any. According to the information of the reporters, there was no DP camp in the British zone where one could get free board and lodgings until one could emigrate, but there were some in the American zone. And there was some hope that the three of us might be accepted.

Blessed reporters! They did not tell us where the camps were, but advised us how to find some kind of relief committee dealing with the refugee problem. Who would have thought then that, years afterwards, I should meet one of these journalists who put us on the right track, in London of all places? It was a great surprise when I then recognized him as the well-known drama critic and theoretician, Martin Esslin.

We were pleased to see that the committee was run by our compatriots. At last, after nearly two months, this was the end of secrecy. We could now learn something more definite about our prospects. The discussion was a mixture of comedy, tragedy and farce. The officials laughed heartily at our naivety, and we tried hard to conceal the shock at hearing the bare truth about our chances. What we had heard sounded incredible, but there was no reason to mistrust these compatriots whose information was based on experience and who did their best to make the sad facts as palatable as possible.

"America? Oh, yes, you can get there in about three years' time after registration, or in two-and-a half if you are lucky. That's how our quota stands now. Register? Why, you must get through the American screening first before you are placed in a DP camp; only then can you do something about your registration."

Stan, who wanted to go to America, jumped up as if every minute counted to bring him nearer his goal. Speaking to Tom and me, the officials were most surprised to meet someone who preferred another country to America. "Everybody goes there, you know? It's the simplest way from this zone. Oh, no, the Americans won't object to your going to England, but, heaven only knows if and how you will get there. You see, nobody wants us, really, and there is no scheme at the moment. There was one not so long ago when Britain took some elderly people who would not have any other chance to emigrate – but there doesn't seem to be any possibility in the near future. It's all very uncertain; you may be lucky to get there next year, or you may have to wait for several years, or you may not get there at all. To be on the safe side, I would register for the United States and cancel it should you get something earlier than that. Pity, the sponsorship by friends in England isn't allowed any longer. Their willingness to take responsibility for you doesn't entitle you to get an entry visa now. You might get one, though, if you sign a contract to work in England as domestic help for four years."

As we were listening, our minds were full of combinations and permutations of how to get the best, or rather the quickest, way out of these dreary possibilities. It was soothing to hear about the old people's scheme; an act of humanity, if not friendship, gave us new hope. We wished to earn our living honestly and be useful in every way; but why should one work for four years in a household? Why not three, or one, or five, or why not in another job? Couldn't one be more useful in the field where one was trained? Four years is a long time, but shorter than the biblical Jacob's seven that he had to serve to deserve his beloved Rachel... Anyway, where there's a will there's a way – perhaps a stiff regulation can be softened in individual cases, especially if our English friends were ready to help. Incorrigible optimists we were! How many more blows would we have to take to see the situation clearly?

The next step was to find the American intelligence service, to be screened again. How long would that take? At the relief committee we were given a very vague reply to this question. "It all depends! It may be very short because you have already been screened by the British, or it may take some time, for, coming from one zone to another makes you more suspicious, or some of the Americans may be jealous that you went to the British first and keep you longer only to show their superiority." It was definitely not "short"; whichever of the two remaining, was difficult to say. The fact remained that it took over two months.

After the experience of Vienna, the screening seemed easier, but perhaps we were hardened? We may have been used to this sort of questions or the Americans may have been more straightforward than the reserved British. The rumours that flashlights were used during the interrogation proved untrue in our case ; there was nothing shocking or distressing, except that it seemed to me that America had not sent their best-mannered people to perform this task. For the first time in my life (and I had been interrogated by my communist compatriots, too) a young man spoke to me, sitting on the opposite side of his desk with his legs on top of it, one stretched towards the north, the other to the south (or east and west?); the view of his large, newly re-soled shoes, with their owner's head bobbing in the middle farther back, was not particularly attractive. It was also for the first time in my life that some of my letters were given to me without envelopes with the remark that someone wanted to have the stamps. On the other hand, these people were quite friendly, more open and personal, acting in a business-like way: you give us your interesting news – so far as it was still news – and we shall feed you, send you to a camp and even admit you to our country if we find you worthy of it. Obviously, Tom and I were gradually becoming more and more shockproof; in any case, we did not feel squeezed like lemons to be thrown away after use.

The US intelligence service was housed in a large modern building. Not very handsome from the outside, but neat, bright and comfortable inside. The greatest features were clean, polished parquet floors, large windows and even hot and cold water in every room which was shared by about six persons. Wide staircases and a spacious hall with a bar where the indispensable Coca-Cola and chocolate could be bought (if one had the money) left a pleasant impression. The number of refugees here was very much larger than in Vienna and it was almost impossible to get acquainted with all of them. Also, the past experience taught us not to talk more than necessary to new people, so we kept together without trying to make friends with the other inmates. Some of them were quite interesting: a young student, our compatriot, turned out to be a very decent and friendly person who joined our trio later on in our enterprise; we spent nine months in the same place and kept in touch with him after he had left for the United States.

Another of our compatriots, a dark-skinned barber with a mop of thick, black, curly hair, had a marvellous gift of story-telling. He would sit with half-closed eyes, entertaining his listeners for hours, telling them, for instance, a story in three parts, of how successfully he was courting a young foreign lady, pretending that he was a famous Italian conductor; or a true story, also in three parts, of how he tried to cross the frontier twice before and how he was caught and imprisoned both times. The third part of the story was to come true only after the completion of his screening, when he meant to cross the Iron Curtain back again and bring over his wife and child. This was, of course, very dangerous and perhaps impossible, although another person cherished a similar idea: to my dismay, a young married woman confided to me that she had escaped with her lover, but that she intended to go back to fetch her little girl who now legally belonged to the deserted husband.

Getting through the Iron Curtain to the eastern side and back seemed an awfully hazardous game, but, apparently, in some cases, corruption made success possible. Some of the frontier guards could still be bribed at that time, but on the other hand the "incorruptible" ones were sometimes shot or wounded by refugees who were forced to fight their way through. But it was still beyond our imagination how whole families with children could manage to get across the Iron Curtain; there were two instances which proved that it was possible. The youngest refugee here was a boy of about three, a very musical child, who expressed his joy of the new freedom by running along the corridors, singing folk songs in his silvery, tinkling little voice, of which he knew a surprising number for his age. Quite often his smiling face was decorated by chocolate up to his ears.

Yes, believe it or not, even chocolate was on the menu sometimes. Altogether, a materialist might not have minded staying here
even for a longer time, because we lived in comfort, with good and
plentiful food. I remember the UNRRA tins from two or three years
after the war. They were a real boon for everybody in my impover-
ished country, but especially as a fast food for students. How
welcome they were now, after the hungry fortnight in the quarantine camp! For the first few days the heavier food made me a bit sick,
but soon my stomach recovered and I regained my normal weight.
The meals were served in a simple and democratic manner: officers
and refugees, all in one dining room, queued with the large self-
service trays for their meals and sat at the same tables.

The screening itself did not take much of the time spent in this
place. During the day, until 5 p.m., all the inmates had to stay in to
be available if needed. After 5 p.m. we were free and could explore
the town or bring books to read, borrowed from an American public
library. In the town itself there was not much to see. Half of it, and
probably the more picturesque and interesting half, was forbidden
to us, as it belonged to the Russian zone; there were only a few nice
spots to be seen in the American zone. Being so near the Russian
zone, one could expect to be followed by someone of the intelligence service, to make sure that one did not communicate with spies
from the other side. On the other hand, one might easily be picked
up in the street and packed into a car and taken back to the Russian
zone. Fortunately, none of the three of us was suspected by the
Americans or considered important by the Russians, so we had no
bad experience in this respect, but we did hear about a Czech politi-
cian who was kidnapped.

On one occasion I wished particularly to go out alone, without
being observed. A kind friend from Switzerland expressed her joy
at my successful escape by sending me a parcel of clothes. They were
all far too big for me, but I hoped to alter them, except for two pairs
of shoes which, I knew, I would never be able to wear, as they were
about three sizes too big for me. Knowing now that, if ever I was to
get to England or anywhere else, I would need money for the
journey; by selling the shoes, I could start saving. I had never been
to a second-hand dealer's before; in spite of my empty pocket, I
found it very embarrassing to go there and be, perhaps, even
observed. Three times I started, three times I turned back. Only on
the fourth time did I pluck up enough courage and later came out of

the shop with a few shillings in my hand. Alas, that wouldn't take me very far and some other way would have to be found.

While staying with the intelligence service we were not allowed to send any applications to emigrate. This could be done only from the DP camp. The second month, the three of us were hardly needed and we wondered why we were not sent there as expected. Soon we found out that being kept longer was actually a favour. The officers knew about life in the camp and thought that we would have preferred to stay with them in comfort. This, however, was far from our wish. Material comfort could not compensate us for the freedom to do something about our emigration, at last. If nothing else, we could register for America and shorten the time of waiting by a few days. Yes, every day, every hour mattered, which would cut down the enforced stay in Austria. By the end of the second month the three of us expressed the wish to leave for the camp and were soon released.

Camp again! Not a very cheerful prospect, but at least this one, on the outskirts of Wels, had no fence or barbed wire around and one had a distinct feeling of freedom here. The place looked like a little village whose inhabitants ceased to care about the appearance of their dwellings and surroundings. The huts were very much in the style of the first camp, only they were more numerous and also a good deal larger. There was a washroom in each of them, placed somewhere in the middle – unfortunately, just one for both men and women.

But, alas! There was no accommodation for me! In the only room occupied by single women all the beds were taken, and a room which had been recently vacated by a family lucky enough to emigrate was securely locked by the manager. He was expected to be absent from the camp for a few days. In this emergency, a kind, decent family offered to take me in their room; the little boy could sleep with the father for the few nights so that I could have his bed. I did not have any illusions about camp life, but this situation brought new surprises for me. It was comforting to know that this family could be trusted and I was grateful for their offer. Seeing the other inhabitants of the camp, the prospect of being put in a room all alone appeared quite dangerous, after what I saw the first night in the camp.

No bugs troubled me, the mattress was fairly even and not too prickly, and my room-mates very quiet, but after a couple of hours of sleep I was woken up by a terrible bang and clatter of broken glass which fell right on top of me. Strangely enough, the little boy, used to such noises, kept on sleeping soundly. And neither of his parents became agitated. They got up quietly, shook the glass from my blanket and looked out of the window for the culprit. "Sorry that it should have happened just the first night you are here," they apologized. "But don't mind that! It's really nothing, we get this here quite often – you see, people just get drunk and then they don't know what they are doing . . . Let's hope that this is all for this night."

Unfortunately, it was not. The drunkard passed by without being interested in who slept under the broken window, but obviously some of his room-mates came out to get him to bed before he could do more harm. Now the most furious argument and fight took place between the two parties. Soon half of the camp was up; the fighters used their knives; some of them were bleeding; the police van arrived, a few warning shots were heard. Four men were put into the van and then at last, the camp was quiet again.

The day was full of activity. First thing in the morning we invaded the office to get all the details necessary for the registration to emigrate to the United States. At least, some sort of hope that we might be able to leave this place some time; actually, however distant, this hope was quite promising, as all the three of us could comply with the two essential conditions, namely, no previous membership in the communist party, and no sign of tuberculosis in the lungs. For those who could not fulfil these two conditions, the US was closed for ever, as were many other countries. Those states who would tolerate either a previous communist (whose membership may not have been voluntary, anyway) or a TB person, were inaccessible for them for other reasons such as language difficulties, lack of contacts or schemes.

With the minimal possibilities of finding a permanent job in Austria, what was the prospect for such people? Permanent stay in the camp, despair, loneliness, occasional little odd jobs which would fetch a few shillings to be spent on drink . . . When there was no money and the despair could not be drowned in drink, thefts and burglaries were attempted; the police would come, put the person to trial and to prison. What did it matter? Prison or camp – there was not much difference between them. If the person could not get out of this cycle to start a new, better life, why should one bother to keep one's register clear of charges? Nothing mattered, really, nothing.

Some of the rooms in the camp were occupied by families who had been waiting for emigration for years. The father might have had a chance to get a job in another country; in some cases, he went alone and his family followed later, after he had proved that he was able to look after them. Sometimes, he preferred to stay in the camp because his child had developed TB and would not be admitted to the prospective country.

In a couple of days the manager came and gave me the key of the empty room where I was to move. Was this called a room to live in? Perhaps it was because it had four walls – but this was the only qualification to this title. There were some primitive bedsteads, or rather, remnants of something which might have born the name in the past: November is a cold month in Austria and a few pieces of firewood would make any room more cheerful; consequently, as soon as anybody left the camp for good, the room was invaded and anything useful was collected and utilized. Apart from the pieces of the bedsteads for firewood, the planks which supported the straw mattress on the bed came in useful to make another bed more even and comfortable; an extra bit of straw made it still more comfortable; an extra chair in the room would provide a seat for the fourth player in a game of cards which shortened the lonely hours.

The result of all this was that I spent one of the worst nights of my life there. I had to sleep on the floor which, fortunately, was a wooden one, not just soil, on a sack with hardly any straw in it. One of the bedsteads was fairly sound, but there were no planks in it to support the straw mattress. Luckily, I could lock myself in, so that the drunkard who banged on the door with all his might at midnight could not get in. But, other doors in the hut were attacked in the same way and shouts and curses were heard. Obviously, some of the men became violent under the influence of drink, and the only defence for me against them was to keep silent and pretend that the room was empty.

After a few days a new family came into the camp and my "room" had to be vacated for them. How they slept on the broken beds, I don't know; meanwhile an extra bed was erected for me in the single women's dormitory, which was certainly an improvement in my standard of living. This room even had a tiny, primitive wardrobe and a wash-bowl! This latter luxury meant also the reduction of my frequent journeys to the river – about half-an-hour's walk distant from the camp – the river being a much more private place for keeping oneself clean than the washrooms in the barracks. The river water was colder as one could expect in October/November, but as long as it was not freezing and the water was flowing, one could get used to these refreshing baths.

The friendly behaviour of my three female room-mates was a pleasant change – that is, as pleasant as it could be in the circumstances. However, it was only a few days later that I heard from my two friends that one of them had a chance to emigrate, meaning that she was healthy and had her police register free of charges of prostitution or other misbehaviour. In fact, she was expected to emigrate soon, and very wisely, too, because her personal records might not be so spotless for much longer, after one of the male camp inmates of dubious reputation had boasted – rightly or wrongly – about his successful courting of her.

The camp was full of rumours, but no one knew exactly the story of the little hairdresser, one of the remaining two. She must have been in the camp for quite a long time, but did not seem to have lost her spirits. Obviously, her imagination was constantly at work, making new projects and schemes, for which activity she was known in the camp and which kept her going. One day she would describe her prospective life in Canada; a few days later she would set off for an imaginary journey to New Zealand; next week she would think that Venezuela was the country of her heart's desire. What a help to have such an imagination! Unfortunately, none of her projects seems to have come true and everybody was convinced that it never would. Let's hope that she did not have to stay in the camp too long; or, if she did, may she not have exhausted all the countries where her fantasy took her. Otherwise, if her optimism had faded, she might have looked just like the other despairing human shadows in the camp.

The third girl's story, which might do for a banal novel, was no secret in the camp. If the little hairdresser was a suspected prostitute, this mundane beauty was an unmistakable one. She had many boyfriends even among the camp inmates – probably her rates were not too high – and she had always some chocolates or sweets in her pocket which she shared generously. There were no traces in her appearance of the poor camp food (it was only a shade better here than in the quarantine camp), as she always had some means of supplementing it; in fact, a tit-bit usually helped to raise her low spirits. It was sheer materialism on which her life was wrecked. As an attractive and fairly well educated girl, she married an American officer stationed in Europe during and after the last war. This, obviously not very handsome millionaire, took her to the United States shortly after the end of the war, but divorced her after a year because of her secret double life of promiscuity. She returned to her Czech home and missed all the previous material comfort bitterly. Prostitution helped to supplement her insufficient earnings. Meanwhile the communists took power and she felt that the later she left things, the more difficult it would be for her to get back to the United States, the country of her heart's desire. So she set her eye on a young, rich jeweller whom she seduced, and made him escape from the communist country with her. No doubt, he loved her without suspecting her scheming, but, for her, he was a mere tool for carrying out her wishes. In Austria she deserted him and, expecting a baby by him (or so she made him believe), felt entitled to steal all the jewels he was able to take with him. She knew how much an abortion may cost, because this was her ninth.

I refused to believe all this. Surely, if people have not enough to do, their imagination wanders in all sorts of crooked ways. Unfortunately, this strange character took a fancy to me and was very kind. She seemed to see something almost saintly in me and imagined that I might plead for her somehow after I had emigrated. She had no scruples whatsoever in confiding to me all about her past which was worse than the incredible rumours. *What* a lesson for me . . . The only hope for this lost character was the possibility that her former husband might forgive her and take her back. She wrote to him many times; there was some money in his first reply, but only bitterness and reproach in the second, and then no more replies came. What was she to do?

How could a newcomer like myself give advice? I had no idea how I was going to get away from this place myself – how could I help people whose situation was so hopeless? At the moment, my only chance was to get to the United States in some two-and-a-half or three years; but something *must* crop up before that – the prospect of spending such a long time among prostitutes was horrifying.

As I had left my country with Tom, we both felt some responsibility for each other and, consequently, set to work together.

Addresses of people who might help were collected, masses of letters written and most of our money spent on postage. A few reporters still came and paid us, replacing the cash we had just spent so that more letters could be written and sent off.

Entry into Britain seemed to be closed for us more than any other country, so, to be on the safe side (how precarious this "safe" side was!), other countries should be tried, too. Any would be better than the camp . . . but, if one still hoped to get to Britain eventually, perhaps one should not go too far away from Europe . . . France, Holland, Denmark, Belgium, Sweden, Norway, Italy, Switzerland, Luxemburg, Iceland. All the crowned heads of Europe received letters from us containing a humble plea to accept two refugees who would be prepared to work in their country. This being done, all of a sudden, the empty days were filled with expectation. Long hours of waiting every day in front of the camp office where the post was distributed were not rewarded with a letter for some time. One had to be patient . . .

During the day one could escape from the camp and spend time in the reading room of the public library. Unfortunately, the camp was situated a good forty-five minutes' walk out of the town; we could not afford to miss the lunch in the camp – such as it was – so it meant two journeys, quite often in rain and mud. Soon the only pairs of shoes we possessed started protesting. The camp cobbler would repair them free of charge, but what to put on in the cold November while he was repairing them? The camp manager had to be asked for help. He took us, with a number of other refugees, into a large barn at the back of the camp where heaps of cast-off clothing were stored, to be handed out to the needy camp inmates. "Take as much as you like," he said. "People don't seem to think much of these things – and, anyway, you will probably find that it is all either too small or too big, as the more common sizes have gone by now."

Being small, I was lucky. There was a good, almost new skirt for me, a winter coat – rather a short, 1942 model – but warm and not too worn, two nightdresses (fancy having a nightdress again!), a couple of petticoats, a hand-knitted bed jacket (which I remade eventually into a handsome jumper) and a beautiful, almost new woollen dressing gown. Believe me, a dressing gown in a DP camp was a ridiculous garment, but, obviously, no-one thought that it could be turned into a good dress. Never mind that I had to wait to carry out this plan for a while, until I could spare the few shillings to buy a needle and a reel of cotton. Only, the most needed shoes were a real problem. The high-heeled pairs were too big for me and useless in the mud and slush. In the end I found a worn-out pair of children's shoes; they were my size, and perhaps the cobbler could repair them, even if he could hardly restore their original shape. The heels were trodden down towards the outside, as if the previous owner did not walk straight. However, better something than nothing!

Stockings were a greater problem. As they are comparatively cheap, none of the kind ladies who sent all these clothes imagined that someone could be so poor as not to be able to buy a pair of stockings. There was not a single pair in the large storeroom and the socks I had found there certainly would not do for the hard, frosty Austrian winter which was rapidly approaching. What to do? A jeweller in the town exploited the situation and offered a ridiculously low price for my gold necklace – and I had to accept it. It was just enough to buy a pair of ugly, cotton stockings which would be warmer than silk or nylon ones.

Having increased my property by the few recently acquired pieces of clothing, the question arose how to carry them when leaving the camp; they could not be packed into my tiny knapsack. Gradually I found out that certain necessities could be acquired by mere co-operation between the refugees themselves. Stan proved to be the most practical of our trio: he gave me a suitcase as a reward for my unpicking an old knitted blanket and making a pullover for him of this material; the suitcase belonged originally to a woman who happened to have two. But she needed a pair of trousers for her young boy more than the other suitcase. Eventually, Stan got the trousers for her from a man in the town whom he helped to chop a heap of firewood. Rightly, Stan was quite proud of his contribution to the general happiness, however ephemeral it might be.

It was just about two months since the three of us arrived at the camp and nothing had happened which would enable us to leave it. Some replies to our applications had arrived, but they did not bring any change for the better. Some were negative, some of them expected our acquaintances to find work for us first - which, of course, was the same as if they were negative; some of them regretted that they were unable to help and gave new addresses to which we might apply. Many more letters were written, more waiting and more disappointment followed.

Only once did a spark of hope twinkle among the black prospects. The relief committee advised other relief committees about us and a reply came from France, saying that they had found work for us in Paris. It was very urgent to act quickly and come at least for an interview: "If you cannot come within ten days, all is lost. Never mind the passport formalities; if you cannot get the documents quickly, try to come without; once you are here, we shall be able to put it right."

This sounded rather dangerous, as we did not wish to spoil our clean record; and yet, too good to be true – what to do? It was risky, but it would mean an end of living in the same room with prostitutes . . . Unfortunately, there was no money for the journey – and hitch-hiking was not known to us then. In the critical moment I turned to friends in Italy (geographically nearest to Austria) who had previously sent me some money for postage. No reply came. I could not understand why these people had broken off with me because of this SOS request. Much later I learnt that a plea for a loan was taken as an offence. They, too, believed that it was not wise to trust refugees whose future was so unpredictable. So the opportunity in Paris was lost and all hope for leaving the camp in the near future thus vanished.

Chapter V

To Innsbruck (French zone)
efforts to secure some existence
frustrated attempts to move on
hope for settling in Eire

Christmas was approaching rapidly. Were we to spend our first Christmas in exile in this desolate place? I am glad to say that we did not, although our position improved only marginally.

One cold and rainy afternoon, a young Catholic refugee-priest, member of a holy order, visited the camp. He came to console those in despair and to look for those for whom there was still hope. He had heard of former students being in the camp; were they interested in continuing in their studies or research while they were forced to remain in Austria? If it had been four months ago, we would have thought it hardly worthwhile for the short period before our emigration. By now we knew better and the suggestion that we might attend lectures, seminars and libraries at the University of Innsbruck sounded like a dream.

The only problem was the material side of the enterprise. Leaving for a university town would mean giving up the only security the camp offered, namely, free board and lodgings, such as they were. Were we prepared to leave it and run a bit more risk in exchange for getting back to university life? Of course we were! Never mind that there were no grants for refugee students; we would be freed from the duty of paying the fees – and that was helpful. There was also the prospect of a student-refugee organisation to be founded shortly, which might be able to deal with our problems. Until then we would have to manage somehow.

The decision was easy enough and, in a couple of days, the trio, or rather a quartet, as Joe, a mathematician, gladly joined us, were on our way. We had to pass Salzburg; why not take the opportunity and look at the place for a couple of hours? It may be our only chance . . . The autumn music festival was just on and we left with the regret that *The Marriage of Figaro* was on the programme in the evening, but we could not afford to watch it. Our few shillings could not possibly be spent on opera tickets and, besides, what a sight our group would be! One of us in his best, dark suit, leaking shoes and rucksack on his back, or me in my "new" coat, 1942 model, in the shapeless children's sports shoes, with a little knapsack on my back, a small suitcase in one hand and a battered cardboard box in the other . . .

Innsbruck, when we reached it in the evening, gave us rather an unpleasant, cold and sleety welcome. The priest, Father Joseph, met us at the station, but it was late and not much could be done that evening. The boys retired to a hut adjoining the station; it was meant for travellers who had to wait overnight for their train connections, and they could get a bed, or rather a bunk, for a very small fee. Although Protestant, I was taken for the night to a Catholic girls' hostel where I was kindly accepted for one or more nights free of charge, until I could find another, more permanent place. The girls in the hostel were mainly teenagers and it was against the practice to accept a woman of my age as a permanent boarder; besides, their parents had to pay for their upkeep, a sum which I could not possibly hope to raise even if I were lucky enough to find a job.

The next few days proved that Father Joseph had been rather too optimistic about the speed with which the student organisation could start operating, and we had come too early to benefit. Still, we had not enough money to return to the camp, so we had to hope to survive somehow. Poor Father Joseph, who felt responsible for us, ransacked all possible charity organisations in the town to get some contribution, but with very little success. All his own, very humble means, went towards the upkeep of our unfortunate group who, of course, were looking for jobs, however temporary, to help. He paid for the bunks in the rail station hostel where the boys stayed the nights; every evening he came, the pockets of his monastic habit contained more than half of his own supper and all the scraps he could collect from the tables of his richer Austrian fellow-priests. But after a few days he found that he had not enough money to buy a stamp for an important letter.

Fortunately, this state of affairs did not last long. I am glad to say that I was the first to relieve the worry of Father Joseph. Through the Students' Union I found a lady who offered free lodgings to a girl-student in return for help in the household. No food and no money, but at least a roof over my head! Actually, this happened on the third day after our arrival from the camp. I felt very independent, although I knew that the few shillings in my pocket would not provide me with essential food for more than a few days. For a week I lived on a daily ration of three rolls which I bought, and a cup of "coffee" in the morning which my landlady offered to me; but after that the situation was resolved!

The local relief committee obtained a grant to be used for the upkeep of students, which enabled the boys to live in a cheap student hostel on the outskirts of the town. Their food was paid for by the new organisation for refugee students. In the meantime, Tom, a good linguist, got a job in an Allied-Powers office, which gave him a very modest, but complete, independence. Consequently, his share from the relief committee could be used to increase the grants for the rest of the group.

As holders of a special grant, however small, we were expected to attend lectures at the University and to sit examinations in due course; here my domestic job prevented me from fulfilling the first obligation, as most of the lectures were held in the morning – and I had to work for the landlady from 8 a.m.–1 p.m. Obviously, some other solution would have to be found, as I was anxious to attend the lectures; besides, I would lose the grant if I did not.

In fact, the arrangements between my landlady and myself were not altogether satisfactory. The elderly spinster was an Austro-Italian, with little, cunning and suspicious eyes; she lived in a large rented house, where, in order to increase her income, she took 4–5 male students as lodgers. Heaven knows whether she needed to do that; although she lived in a very poor, uncomfortable way, she still looked like a living image of Mrs. Beetle from Čapeks' *The Insect Play*. Instead of rolling her ball of dirt, her precious capital, she carried a little suitcase everywhere, even to the bathroom and lavatory, and the little key to it was constantly dangling on a string round her neck. Her bedroom was locked night and day and I was not allowed to clean it. She herself did not do any cleaning: what might the bedroom look like? Probably very much like the bedlinen, which seemed never to be changed, of the poor lodgers. Its colour was exactly the same as the floor before I washed it for the first time! Making the beds every morning made me sick and frightened me in my nightmares long afterwards.

The house itself was rather large and could have been a lovely nobleman's residence in the past. Now, it was turned into an enormous grubby, grey, gloomy icebox. The only fire in the house was the huge tiled stove in the kitchen, which, owing to its large size and cold, tiled floor, never got properly warm. To feel the warmth one had to sit on the ledge of the stove, or lean against it. What a sight to see the landlady, sitting huddled on the ledge of the stove, with her hand on the indispensable little suitcase, and the 4–5 students, with books or drawing boards on their knees around her, like chickens under the wing of a hen!

In this frosty December I used to see this scene every evening when I came "home" from the student club which was now operating; not only the feeding facilities, but also a pleasant club room had been opened, with periodicals, newspapers and even a piano! The place was run by a Jesuit, Father Pierre, who was previously an army priest. With the support of UNESCO and other organisations he enabled the refugee students to continue at the University and also to have a centre where they could feel at home, among people in the same predicament.

Father Pierre was most efficient and practical. He managed to find the means for carrying out his great idea; he had also a good imagination. A large, modern house which might have served as a military office in the war, was converted into a pleasant club house. The groundfloor was used as a club room and offices. The basement, which might have been previously an air-raid shelter, was made into a spacious kitchen and a number of small dining rooms. The first floor became Father Pierre's and his secretary's rooms, and the attics were turned into accommodation for the staff – all neat and labour-saving.

The number of refugee students and postgraduates in the district was larger than Father Pierre anticipated. There was a mix of nationalities. Some students had already settled down for good, having found adequate jobs, though none were so well off as to be excluded from the membership and benefits of this new organisation. Apart from the club facilities it provided also very substantial lunches and dinners for members for a modest charge. The prosperity of this enterprise was secured by Father Pierre's skill and co-operation between him and the refugees who provided him with a very cheap staff. Having no other possibility to earn their living, they were glad to accept jobs which would secure board, lodgings and a few shillings of pocket money. Tasks and duties could be carried out so that there would still be a chance to attend lectures and seminars at the university. I was very glad when I was offered this in return for washing up the dishes after the meals and helping to clean the dining rooms. It did not matter that, being employed, I had lost the relief committee grant; that could always be recovered if I happened to lose this job. It meant farewell to the filthy sheets in the Austro-Italian icebox! Now, I was sharing one of the small attic rooms with another girl who also worked in the kitchen. I washed the rubber-covered floors in the dining rooms at 7 a.m., attended lectures during the morning, laid the tables before the meals, wiped a dozen or so tables after them and washed about 240–250 plates, cups and saucers, as well as the cutlery, every day. There were no dishwashers then.

Actually, it was the cutlery rather than the heaps of plates which frightened me in my dreams then. The chef insisted on my using a lot of detergent for the washing up, so that one could not see through the soapy water; as he used to throw the carving knives straight into the sink, I had to fish them out; my fingers were cut very often, sometimes quite dangerously. But even that was much better than making beds in the Austro-Italian lady's icebox . . .

We spent our first Christmas in exile in the student-refugee club. Father Pierre insisted on having a party, so that we could feel more at home; I dreaded such an occasion. It was no use trying to be cheerful when our hearts were sore enough. Still, we had to conform and even provide some entertainment; we could not disappoint Father Pierre who meant so well. Fortunately, Tom was very musical and had a good, rather deep and full bass voice; Stan had an extremely clear and pleasant tenor, but a doubtful musical ear; so it was mainly Tom who provided the programme, singing arias from Czech operas. From me, as the only "pianist", they expected piano solos! I have always been very nervous when playing in public and here there was an additional problem – the total lack of sheet music and, of course, the long interval without practising. Perhaps one could manage something not too ambitious if one had the music – but I could not play by heart. So, somebody suggested borrowing something from the local music school, forgetting that refugees, as a caste, were generally mistrusted and that such a scheme was likely to fail. Still, I was prepared to leave my watch as a surety, as my "identity" card was hardly sufficient proof of my honest intentions. What a surprise when the headmaster of the music school lent me some Dvořák and Smetana before I could make my offer! This was the strongest impression which marked my first Christmas in exile: if he had given me the music, it would have been out of charity, but he lent it to me without any guarantee, which meant that I was trusted, considered as a human being, not branded as a refugee!

My daily duties took me about seven hours a day and there was still some time left for letter-writing; both Tom and I kept on hoping that we might speed up our move to Britain somehow. Though, whatever might happen, it was clear to us that our saving for the journey would take many months if it continued at the present rate. My pocket money was about fifty shillings per month and Tom could not save more than that from his earnings either. Yet, now having a more permanent address perhaps this was the right time to get in touch with my uncles in London. Our family had lost touch with them after their departure, as their correspondence with them, in the communist Czechoslovakia, would mark the uncles too obviously as enemies of the régime and the family would have suffered for it. British intelligence officers had found their addresses for me already in Vienna where we were not allowed any outside contact, but my uncles appeared to be in circumstances which – apart from goodwill, advice and moral support – excluded any means of help to us. Although one was a Professor and the other an army general, now in their sixties, they were lucky to be accepted by Britain as her war-time residents and also under the scheme involving elderly people; they now lived in retirement on grants from the Czech Refugee Trust Fund.

Now that we were in touch again, they did their best to help. Limited as their power was, no stone could be left unturned. The uncles became instrumental in an action which seemed utterly hopeless at first, but which, miraculously, established links that proved vital later. My memory recalls that, shortly after the communist *putsch* in 1948, a short notice on the English departmental notice board at Prague University was offering a modest vacation grant in England for a student of Professor Vočadlo, my first and dear supervisor in English. Clearly, nobody could benefit as civilian travel abroad was not permitted. What if something like that still existed? Not likely, after nearly five years ... but perhaps there was no harm in enquiring? How could I find the necessary details? I could remember nothing more than just one name which somehow stuck in my memory as Professor Vočadlo casually mentioned it at a small tea party in his home in 1948, to which I was invited: the name was Bradbrook . . . It was familiar to me in connection with Shakespeare and Elizabethan studies, but, somehow, Professor Vočadlo's remark connected it in my memory also with this vacation grant.

My uncle found Dr. Muriel Bradbrook for me at Girton College, Cambridge. But was she the correct person and if so, would she remember what must have been for her a very minor event nearly five years ago? Feeling rather ridiculous I wrote my enquiry full of apologies, prepared to get yet another negative answer, if any. But it came surprisingly quickly. Negative, of course, what else? They had taken a Polish student instead when no Czech could benefit from the grant, she wrote, but she was always willing to help a student of her friend Professor Vočadlo; would I tell her more about myself? A lively correspondence followed and soon this learned lady became my true guardian angel. She got in touch with my uncles as well as with my friend in Stratford (whom I met in Prague where she lived, married to a Czech army officer before she moved, in 1953, back to Stratford). With a team of a few Girtonians she set to work.

Parcels containing clothes and books arrived and I no longer looked funny in my 1942 model coat which was now replaced by a better-fitting garment. Occasionally also the Americans sent gift parcels to be distributed among refugees, containing two brand-new towels, combs, soaps, hairpins, shaving sticks, razor blades, tooth-brushes and pastes. After the New Year, rather thrilling news came: American charities had raised enough funds so that every refugee could get a new coat, dress or suit, a pair of shoes and a set of under-wear! The head of the relief committee took our group to a large store to make our choices; he was so considerate as to allow us to buy other, more needed things instead of the suggested outfit. By now I was fairly well off with clothes, so my special choice caused great amusement to the rest of the group: smiling happily, I emerged from the store with a large fibre suitcase (remember, I possessed some books now!), containing some stockings and three pairs of shoes, one for the winter, one for the spring and one for the summer. Now I could travel to Britain like a respectable person – no more as an odd-looking eccentric.

The kind friends in England soon found and confirmed that the official British hospitality included a condition that the person in question should sign a contract for four years' domestic service. No,

I was not afraid of domestic work – but four years is a long time for someone who had already lost four years when the Czech universities were closed during the war. By now I was thirty ... Our friends were all too willing to find other jobs for us, but unfortunately no prospective employer would accept us without an interview. How could one get out of this vicious circle? Perhaps one might come as a visitor and make necessary contacts with such employers, but one would have to leave the country after the expiry of the visitor visa, so as not to prejudice the authorities against one in the future. This was the last thing we would have liked to cause, but where would we leave for? Austria? How long would it take us to save for TWO journeys? There was no help for it, we must wait.

As time passed, the atmosphere in the kitchen became less pleasant for me than it had been at the beginning. One of the full-time employees, a non-student, rather a temperamental young man, got drunk several times and was very rude towards everybody. I became his special target as I was now the only woman in the kitchen, after the other girl, an Austrian, was dismissed as a comparatively expensive member of the staff. I had to take over her duties as well, which I found quite taxing, especially with the disturbances caused by the young drunkard. In the end there was nothing else to do but to complain to Father Pierre. Strangely, he seemed to have some weakness for this boy who became nastier still and the protection I had from the students and the other members of staff did not bring sufficient improvement of the situation. The time of the examinations was approaching rapidly, also a visit from one of the sponsors was expected and Father Pierre ordered a spring-cleaning. In a few days the house was spotless and yet, one day I was woken up by Father Pierre at midnight to go and collect a sweet-paper which someone had dropped after I had cleaned the floor. Father Pierre knew how to impose his authority.

A 'flu epidemic ravaged its way through Central Europe. The club rooms were emptier than ever; familiar faces disappeared and then reappeared after some time. The head chef was among the first victims, I among the last. Mine was rather a nasty case and Father Pierre, for all his thriftiness, called a doctor. At the doctor's third visit he found me much better – and my room full of visitors. That is, about three people – because there would not be enough space for more in my tiny room. Yes, believe it or not, I had my *own* room, right under the roof. After the dismissal of my former Austrian room-mate I had to vacate the larger room for two boys and got this tiny one which was, really, an unfinished attic. There was a hard, cement floor and no ceiling; instead, there was a sloping roof covering three-quarters of the room, so that one could stand erect only at the door. Lying in bed, I could easily reach the tiles of the roof, or the tiny skylight which was the only window in the room. Fortunately, it did not leak as skylights tend to do – otherwise I would have been soaked in bed. At one side of the door there was enough space for a miniature, primitive wardrobe and a chair; the new suitcase served as a bedside cabinet, chest-of-drawers, table and bookcase. A towel was used instead of a tablecloth, a little drinking glass borrowed from the kitchen served as a vase which contained some wild flowers collected in the nearby field. How primitive. Yet this little room will always live in my memory as my first place of privacy since leaving my Czech home. Virginia Woolf would have been pleased by my independence, for not only had I a room of my own, but even a key to it!

During my illness an interesting piece of news reached me. One of the refugees who came to visit me told me that he was leaving for Germany and asked if I would like to do likewise. Why to Germany of all places? Was it any better? Obviously, it was. People who were granted the status of refugee were entitled to a very small, but regular income from the government if they had no job; that could give one some sort of security . . . Unfortunately, this lawyer-refugee was very secretive about how to get to Germany and acquire the legal status. Yes, it could be done and he hoped to help me, but he must first try himself; his plan might fail if he made it public. This was tempting, although one could imagine that there would be some risks in return for the advantages; I hesitated to accept this offer of help.

I was still in bed with 'flu when the first card from Germany from him came. Yes, everything worked according to plan, and he would write again. No address was given. Anyway, I had not much faith in the possibility of my getting over the next stage of my odyssey in this way; but I was very interested in how this person was getting on, whether there were some doors open for the refugees, after all. Obviously, there were, but perhaps one had to be a lawyer to find them . The next letter came from Paris, the following from Milan . . . The young lawyer managed to get some sort of grant. Yes, he had to live very modestly, but still, he could live almost like a normal citizen. Of course, having left Germany, he could not help me just at the moment, sorry . . .

Never mind, I did not set my heart on this venture. Soon a letter came from my Stratford friend. It included a formal invitation for official purposes, saying that she would be responsible for all expenses incurred during this visit. Full of joy I read the letter three times without stopping. In the meantime, what about the fare? It would be necessary to leave England after a while . . .

Tom came for lunch at the club, but that was the busiest time for me and I could not tell him till after 6 p.m. when his shift was over. "Hurry to the Consulate!" he told me without hesitation. He was rather optimistic. The money would be found somehow, perhaps through a loan; and three months, which was the normal validity of a visitor visa, was quite a long time – some solution would be found in the meantime when the case could proceed on a more personal basis. Once in the country itself, everything should be easier, we imagined. So far, all the refugees we met wished to go to the United States; surely, British authorities would not refuse one or two in their country, if they could properly interview them? We were confident that we had something to offer.

The next day I applied for the visa. As I had no passport, some sort of travel document would be issued, once the visa was granted. All this would take some time, I was told – and that would give me plenty of time to get ready. If this had been merely a question of packing, I could have been at the station in an hour's time – but there was the problem of the fare and the examinations. The exams were to be taken shortly and I wished to fulfil my duties. I wrote a long essay for a seminar and passed all the examinations with success in about a fortnight. The relief committee were pleased with the results; in fact, they were quite well disposed even to those who failed, as they realized the difficulties of sitting examinations in a foreign language. Such students were not deprived of their grants if they failed for the first time. I told the committee about the application for the visa and also about my worry with respect to how I would pay the fare. Yes, the committee could make a loan for me. How easy everything seemed to look all of a sudden! Can it be true that I would be able to leave? I was tempted to give notice from my now very difficult job, but not knowing how long all the procedure and formalities might take, I decided that it was too risky. Every penny was more useful now than ever and it would be only wise to work till the end. Father Pierre was accustomed to see the refugees coming and leaving suddenly; he would not mind if I left only at a short notice.

Six weeks passed and there was no sign of the visa. Only after seven weeks did a letter come from the Consulate. The visa was refused! I read this information several times in disbelief. Surely, there must be a mistake? No explanation, no reason was given. Why should it be refused? I ran to the Consulate. The consul was out, the secretary did not know any details, sorry. Yes, they would write and make an appointment for me.

Another week passed and no letter arrived. Obviously, this case was considered finished by the Consulate and they had no intention of considering it any further. I wrote asking for an explanation. The relief committee prepared me for the worst. Yes, I would get a reply eventually, but I must not expect miracles; the case is finished, no doubt.

They were right. Through a letter I was coolly informed that I intended to enter Britain under false pretences and nothing more could be done. What did they mean? Why should I be accused of something I was far from committing? This friend of mine in Stratford was a most respectable person and she was prepared to take responsibility for me; why should we be mistrusted? I did not mean to trespass by working those three months as I was over-anxious to avoid anything illegal; was meeting a few more people in England illegal, too? I was deeply hurt. Yes, it is possible that, in the past, some refugees may have been admitted to the country and became nuisance there – but why should the same be expected from everybody, without any discrimination? Of course, for the officials, the name of a stranger on an application form did not mean more than the paper itself; why should they be bothered? My academic degree was usually respected as a mark of integrity; perhaps if I had been granted an interview with the consul the result might have been different . . . But, no, I was no beggar, I was not going to deal with people who mistrusted me. I swallowed the bitter pill almost with tears in my eyes and wrote to my friend, thanking her for all she had done for me. It was with deep regret that I would not be able to see her in her country.

What to do next? Wait for two years to get to the United States? That seemed to be the only possibility still open. Spring was just around the corner. Nearly a year away from home and still drifting.

High in the mountains snow was glistening in the lovely sunshine, skiers enjoyed their last trips up in this season. I joined a group of students on my day off to get to the top of one of the highest peaks in the neighbouring Alps. None of us possessed skies or high boots – and in the flimsy walking shoes we could not get anywhere, except by the funicular. Even on top of the mountain we could not walk much, apart from a narrow path round the summit. But we could lean against the hardened snowdrifts, turn our faces to the sun and watch, half-sitting, half-standing, the marvellous view. How peaceful, how quiet it was there! The world could be pleasant if only there was less mistrust and hatred among people . . .

On my return to the kitchen duties a letter was waiting for me, with the address written in an unknown, very neat handwriting. The content, I realized on second reading, amounted to a tentative marriage proposal. A compatriot who used to pay me attention in my native town, informed me that he managed to escape from communist Czechoslovakia a few months earlier, that he had a good job in Germany, and that he had the possibility of emigrating to Canada before long. He had heard that I was in exile and had tried to find me, wondering what were my plans? If I had nothing better in view, would I like to come to Germany and discuss whether we could make a joint enterprise and perhaps settle down, later on, near each other, in order not to be quite so alone among strangers?

I was so surprised that I could not immediately recollect who the writer of the letter was. But I soon realized that I knew him as a very decent person and that his offer could not be but honest. Yet, I had come here with Tom, and although we were just friends, we had made previously a similar pledge and I would feel disloyal. Only, Tom could still hope to get to Britain, while that country was closed for me now. In fact, it could be Tom who might be disloyal if he had the chance to get to Britain – and I could not blame him if he were. It was not likely that he could help me to get over there, too, if British subjects themselves were helpless.

It was actually Tom himself who reminded me of the fact that a proper state citizenship (which would mean an end to all officialdom and difficulties connected with it) could be within easy reach for a girl, through marriage. How could he think that I could sell myself into a marriage of convenience? But some refugees did so, as shown by my camp experiences.

I would have liked a trip to Germany to discuss the new possibilities, but could not imagine how my compatriot there could think of my spending all my savings on it. Was he himself so well off after a few months' time? Besides, how could I get the necessary travel documents? How could I take the risk of possibly losing my kitchen job as a consequence of a few days' leave? No, nothing could be done in the circumstances. Yet, one point of the whole matter surprised me very much: how was it possible that a refugee in Germany could get a well-paid job after only a few months' stay there? How could it be that he had a chance to emigrate so quickly, without having any friends in Canada? That country would take him, employ him and even pay for his journey. Was Canada kinder than other countries towards refugees? Or, was Germany more efficient than Austria in the way of helping refugees to settle? Or, was this person luckier than other refugees? Who could tell? I knew that he was honest and could hardly be more shrewd than Tom or Stan. Having my kitchen job and a roof over my head, such as they were, I thought that I was luckier than many other refugees – and so I was when one remembered those who still lived in the camps. Perhaps more patience was needed ... The chance may still come, especially if this newly-found friend promised to help both Tom and me when he reached and settled in Canada.

Canada? I tried to imagine myself in that country but somehow could not. I did not know so much about Canada as about Britain, but that did not seem to be the reason. Surprised, I caught myself still thinking of Britain, no matter how much I tried to dispel the idea. How foolish! How obstinate! My hurt pride had induced all this, no doubt. They have accused me wrongly, and somehow I was determined to prove it to them.

My English friends encouraged me. No, they were not sure what to do, but there MUST be some way. They hoped to write again soon, but I felt that their words were said only to cheer me up. They may succeed, they may not. I looked regularly at the various notices at the University, out of interest and for possible inspiration. The end of the academic year was near and vacation jobs were advertised. What about trying this fish factory in Sweden? It could not be worse than in the kitchen and perhaps there might be other possibilities in Sweden later on? Of course, the Swedish authorities had Tom's and my name already in their records since the time when we enquired about emigration to that country; a job, they said then, could guarantee the entry visa . . . However, the reply came surprisingly quickly. Sorry, they could accept only Austrian students, no stateless people.

At the same time, there was a spark of hope for Tom. British Railways required porters for the summer! The Austrian student representative was not very hopeful, being afraid, and rightly, too, of more complicated formalities in this individual case than in the case of the Austrians, but he promised to do his best.

While Tom was waiting for a reply, Father Pierre gave us, his kitchen staff, a treat. He had to collect some material from Baden-Baden and, having plenty of room in his minivan, took us for a beautiful three-day trip. We stopped at Munich where I offended Father Pierre by refusing the huge mug of beer which everybody considered a delicacy; but I made up for it when I managed to find the dispersed group in the beautiful park called *Englischer Garten*. We were all shocked when passing the ruins of Karlsruhe, but were relieved after having reached the neat town of Baden-Baden. Still, nothing could beat the beauty of the Alpine mountains, lakes and forests which we saw on the first part of the journey, and we were looking forward to seeing it once more on the way back. That time we saw it in moonlight, which gave the landscape a special dreamy quality. So dreamy that, at the end of the journey, we were all surprised that we were still alive. Father Pierre with his secretary enjoyed themselves somewhere before setting off for the return journey so that his driving, under a strong influence of drink, turned into something like a wild *dance macabre*. Lakes and precipices particularly attracted him, and if it were not for one of the boys who pulled the handbrake a few times at the right moment, our problems could have been solved remarkably quickly.

After this trip conditions in the kitchen deteriorated considerably, at least for me. There was some tension which I could not understand; Father Pierre appeared there more often, as if checking on something, and the temperamental assistant chef got drunk more frequently than before. Naturally, a Frenchman, no matter if a priest, thought a little glass of wine for everybody at dinner was appropriate – and there was always enough of it in the pantry. I disliked the behaviour of the assistant chef intensely; we had arguments, however much I tried to avoid talking to him, knowing that, when he lost his temper, this person could become a wild beast. By the end of the academic year I could not stand it any longer. I explained to Father Pierre, but he obviously sheltered the unruly man who seemed to have held the priest somehow in his power; he accepted my resignation rather than rebuking or dismissing the troublemaker. I could still use the club's facilities on the same terms as the other students, only my room would be needed for my successor.

That could be expected; in fact, I wished to keep away from the club as much as possible. Father Joseph very much approved of my step. He, too, had the feeling that something was going very wrong with the club. He arranged for me to get the relief committee's grant and also to be accepted again in the Catholic girls' hostel as a lodger only. Normally, girls were expected to feed there as well, but my case was not regular. However reasonably priced, it would have still been beyond my means, that is, beyond the relief committee's grant.

Now I occupied half of a cubicle in a large dormitory; my things were put into a locker. Not being a proper resident, I could not use the common room, but that did not really matter. There was the university library, English Seminar, and French Institute where one could read and study. What a freedom all of a sudden! No more washing up, no more scrubbing floors, no more bleeding fingers, no more curses and bad language of the assistant chef, no more fear of Father Pierre's rebuke should he find a flaw in the clean floor! Why had I not left that place earlier? Of course, it was not quite so simple. It was better to be independent, but if ever I was to leave Austria, I would need money. A job was essential even now – but how to find one?

I went to the Labour Office full of hope in spite of the fact that Austrian subjects would always have preference as far as employment was concerned. I knew that I would always be at a disadvantage. Several doors, labelled with names of various types of jobs, led from the main hall. All except one were also labelled "no vacancies". The remaining one, "resident domestic staff", announced that there were ten vacancies, but the queue at this door numbered at least fifty!

Slowly I walked for lunch to the club. There I found Tom talking to Father Pierre and a stranger. I was asked to join the group and was introduced. The stranger, an Allied Powers commissioner, came to offer jobs to a couple of good linguists and Father Pierre could think of no one better than Tom and myself. Apart from the knowledge of certain languages the new employees would have to be absolutely reliable politically; the working hours would be fairly long, but the salaries sounded fantastic – at least, so they seemed to the two of us who were used to working for next to nothing. We would be resident in Germany, starting to work in some four to six weeks' time. Would we like to come for an interview? We looked at each other and agreed, provided that we would not be committing ourselves definitely; we would like to think it over before finally accepting. This right was reserved for both parties concerned.

Does it not look strange that people in our position should hesitate to accept such an opportunity? The fact was that we still hoped to move to the country of our hearts' desire. British Railways were quite willing to deal with all the extra formalities in Tom's case and he hoped that he might find this job useful for his future settling in Britain; also, my friends wrote more hopefully again although they did not tell me exactly what was being done, so that in case of failure I could be spared another disappointment.

And then, there was the high salary which we were offered. Was it not suspicious? Yet, what danger could be behind it? Could someone advise us? Perhaps our compatriot Father Joseph, who had been working among refugees for a number of years, could enlighten us. We confided in him. No, he did not think that there was anything suspicious or dangerous. Employees in such services of high responsibility were generally well paid. The only snag might be the emigration. One never knew when the chance might come and it might look bad and, moreover, suspicious, to leave the job at short notice. Also, since our travel documents would be issued by the Allied Powers, we might find it difficult, or even impossible, to emigrate in case we happened to become indispensable in these jobs.

What to do? No decision had to be taken for several weeks; obviously, our political past at home and in exile had to be examined first. The interview, however, took place quite quickly. Necessary documents for a day's journey across the Austro-German frontier and return tickets were enclosed in the invitation.

The journey was most enjoyable. With so limited financial means we hardly knew how near we were to all these beautiful places we saw from the train. Mountains, rivers, lakes, crevasses, forests, precipices, gorges, meadows, little villages . . . Though, perhaps this lovely spot where we were to live was a little too remote – the salaries would compensate by giving us a comfortable life. But that was not really why we had left our beloved Czechoslovakia! How to decide? On the one hand, there was the precarious possibility of emigrating, connected, surely, with a lot of difficulties, if at all possible; on the other hand, there was the possibility of a comfortable life, perhaps without emigration, and with our freedom limited. We seemed to have stuck to the first like leeches. Thank heaven the decision could be postponed!

The necessity of finding at least some temporary job immediately became more urgent. One day I saw a notice on a hotel door, advertising a temporary job in the hotel kitchen for a few weeks during the busiest summer season. Should I try? How ridiculous that my short practice in the celebrated club kitchen where, in fact, I did hardly any actual cooking, should be a more valuable recommendation than all my university education! Still, it did help and I was accepted. Tom, knowing of my academic inclinations and my distinct indifference towards cooking, found this piece of news most amusing. Though, he had to agree that the earnings which I was going to get as an apprentice in the first year of learning would be useful, as well as the practice in cooking itself.

The prospect of cooking more or less professionally made me both amused and scared, but the consolation that it would be only temporary gave me enough courage to start the next morning. Clearly, if I disappointed their expectations, which was very likely, I would be sacked – but if nothing worse should happen, I was prepared for that.

The secretary who accepted me introduced me to the head chef, informing him that I was a university graduate but that I had some practice in the kitchen (!) and that I agreed to work as an apprentice. The chef's sour face betrayed that he was not impressed; indeed, he was rather doubtful whether I was the most precious acquisition for the busiest season – and quite rightly, too. He was not used to having apprentices of my age and education; in fact, he looked at educated women with suspicion. That was not altogether encouraging. He thanked the secretary as he had to be polite towards his superior, but did not say a word to me. He only gave me a bad-tempered look which seemed to say, "what on earth are we going to do with this strange creature?"

It was most fortunate for both of us that he sent me to work in the department of confectionery, situated in the corner of the huge kitchen, most distant from an enormous cooker. In the first moment I took this as a punishment for some uncommitted crime because the oven was a much greater mystery for me than the top of the cooker – but soon I discovered the advantages of being there and not in the main department, under the head chef himself.

The greatest gain was that my boss, the confectioner, was a polite, quite young person, perhaps only a few years my senior. He seemed to have been very pleased at finding me docile and was the more willing to teach me. Although he was a fast worker, he had enough patience with me and appreciated a nicely decorated cake, no matter if it took me longer to do. The first day he taught me how to make Italian ice cream of which large quantities had to be prepared every day first thing in the morning. This was rather easy and, in a few days, he entrusted the ice cream to me entirely. Fruit salads, cocktails and whipping the cream soon formed part of my duties, too, though I could not take over the actual baking quite so soon: my young boss could not risk any failure. Should something be spoiled, the value of the material would be deducted from his wages. Do you think one could simply throw the spoilt dessert into the dustbin and start all over again? Impossible. Not only that the head chef had his eyes everywhere, but chiefly because the huge, overfilled pantry was always locked and no one, except the manageress, had access to it. Every morning the chef and the confectioner handed her a list of various foodstuffs needed, which were prepared by her in the required quantities. I cannot recall her face any more, but I shall always remember her elegant dark dresses, manicured nails and her miserliness. I can still see her weighing the miserable brawn for the supper of the kitchen staff: each employee was entitled to 100 gram; should the finger of the scales point a shade towards the right, she would not hesitate to cut off a tiny bit which served the only purpose to bring the finger on the scales back to the left.

The staff had their lunches and suppers on the spot. Compared both in quality and quantity with the meals prepared for the guests, they were as if one compared a rose with a cabbage. Yet, apart from the brawn, which, surely, must have been made by the worst butcher in the town, these various *Eintopfgerichts* (hotpots) tasted much better than the camp food, as the professional chefs and cooks knew all the tricks of the trade of how to improve flavour without using costly ingredients. The meals had to be swallowed as quickly as possible; in fact, everything in the kitchen had to be done with the highest speed. I have never found out whether this was really necessary or just a whim or nervousness of the head chef. No doubt, the hotel was very prosperous and the staff was kept busy all the time; perhaps, gradually, the head chef developed a habit of chasing everybody to speed up as a sheer whim of his?

If Father Pierre's manner was that of an army officer, this new chief boss of mine was a born dictator. One word, or just a sharp look, was enough for anyone of the staff to leave everything in order to carry out his new wish. Sometimes, it seemed to me, his wishes were not altogether sensible, and yet the people obeyed him like sheep, as if they had no will or judgement of their own. Of course, losing one's job in Austria at this time was a serious matter and one could not run such a risk – except for a poor refugee who still cherished a hope to get away as soon as possible from this place of tension. How lucky I was compared with these Austrians! I wonder if this fact gave me an air of confidence which the head chef mistook for my inadequate respect for his authority, but I had the impression that he hated me – although we never spoke to each other. In any case, there was hardly any talk in the kitchen, as every superfluous word might hold up the work in process and the chef's obsession of working at top speed infected the staff – out of fear of his anger. His temper certainly did not need to be provoked too much to flare up. Every morning I entered the kitchen, wondering whether this would be my last day there and how much longer I would be able to avoid irritating the chef and being sacked as a consequence.

Strangely enough, nothing disastrous happened for quite a few days; the confectioner had no complaints against me, and, on two Saturdays I was very proud to receive my wages. Then, there was Sunday, the most agreeable day in the kitchen, as agreeable as it could be. The head chef and the confectioner were free on Sundays, most of the meals were prepared on Saturday and the management of the kitchen lay in the hands of one of the more senior cooks – the most competent and skilful cook I have ever met. I shall never forget the speed with which she could manually turn a huge cabbage head or an onion into *hauchdünn* shreds (thin as breath), or how she managed to cook four elaborate dishes at the same time. What would the silly head chef do without her? And yet, she, too, gave me a frightened look when I asked her once for a knife in the presence of the feared boss. But on Sunday everything was different. All the tension had gone, people were human and worked quietly and I even found time to copy some interesting recipes out of the confectioner's book which he lent me as a special favour. They must still be somewhere among my souvenirs.

It was just at the time when my young boss entrusted to me to do some more skilled pieces of work that I got the long expected sack. Actually, I was not dismissed, but I left after this "accident" and so the result was the same. I knew that trouble was bound to come sooner or later, but I thought that some burnt *gateau* was more likely to end my career rather than simple stewed apricots. By now I could stone apricots just as quickly as the confectioner, but the trouble was that they had to be put into water, boiling in a large saucepan on the huge cooker. Some other large saucepans were on the cooker as well, containing various stews, vegetables and other dishes. I felt the head chef's eyes watching every movement of mine; no doubt, he was looking for trouble. What was I to do? Turning over the basket with the apricots into the steaming saucepan with one quick movement would splash the sugary water right into the goulash – and I was bound to be in trouble; perhaps it would be wiser to do it more slowly and without splashing? Unfortunately, this safer way was far from the chef's idea He came running, grabbed the basket, turned it over the saucepan with one fierce movement, resulting in the water being splashed all over the place, some of the apricots fell into the goulash, some on the floor, and the empty basket was thrown into a corner with fury. All this happened in a second and without a word. Evidently, the silence was meant to continue until, as expected, I should have collected the basket and the fruit from the floor and apologized. However, I did not feel guilty, and in my heart of hearts I was rather amused. I had to suppress a giggle. Besides, the ice cream machine needed immediate attention. Consequently, the silence continued longer than expected; in fact, it was never broken as I walked towards the machine, wondering how the guests would enjoy their goulash improved with apricots, and whether all culinary quarters were haunted by bad-tempered, uncivilized boors.

The scene itself did not appear uncommon in this place, only my reaction to it seemed rather unusual; any other girl would have picked up the basket and apologized. The confectioner was truly sorry to hear that I did not intend to come the next day and was quite prepared to intervene if necessary. But I thought it best to leave; not knowing what difficulties might be in store for me in the future, perhaps it was not wise to strain my nerves in this way.

This "accident" helped to put my conscience at rest; at least, it gave me a reason. I did not feel quite so cowardly at leaving that place after barely three weeks. Now I was again where I was before, that is, at the beginning.

The cheerless days continued, and in this period of waiting we were rather shattered by the news that one of our group, a young Slovak, was drowned when bathing in the river. That beautiful, clean and sparkling Inn – but how treacherous! No details were given, and although we did not say so aloud, I am sure the word "suicide" lingered in Tom's mind just as in mine. Yes, it *could* have been misadventure, but we knew that this boy's prospects were not very bright and the long-lasting insecurity could have caused a fatal depression.

Somehow, the event reminded us again of how sadly divided the world was; this person, like the rest of us, although living now geographically not very far away from his Slovak home, could not, of course, communicate with his family. But the fact that he died and his family may possibly never have found out anything about his end, made us feel like stray animals, being knocked about, wanted by nobody. Who would care when we die? Somehow, the situation and feeling of alienation did not make sense in this place surrounded by the magnificent Alps, where the beauty of nature made all misery seem absurd.

Having comparatively enough free time on my hands, I tried to explore the surroundings as much as my pocket and my shoes (which I could not afford to ruin!) allowed me. In doing so, one day I nearly lost my life. It was on a beautiful, sunny day when I took a short bus drive out of the town, wishing to climb one of the lower mountains nearby. Even the lowest was still high enough, but, inexperienced as I was, I thought that it was possible to reach the top and return on the same day. There was a nice footpath and the mountainside looked superb in the sunshine: it was overgrown thickly by Alpine azaleas (*Alpenrosen*) which were just then in full bloom; the scenery was breathtaking.

Surrounded by this beauty I climbed up for hours almost in a trance, without noticing that the path was becoming increasingly overgrown, until I found myself hemmed in up to my waist by these lovely shrubs, unable to see any path at all. A long way down I could see the main road on which the bus came, and decided to descend "as the crow flies". That seemed to me quicker than looking for the path which was not easy to find. Darkness was descending and I had to act swiftly, even at the expense of possible damage to these lovely flowers.

The *Alpenrosen* proved to be tougher than I was. Thick as they grew, they resisted my efforts and did not allow me to pass. The quicker I tried to go forward, the thicker they seemed to be, closing over me. Everywhere was still, not a living soul within sight or sound: crying for help was useless. Eventually the struggle exhausted me and the result of the nervous strain from the past year started showing. I was about to give up and reconciled myself to the possibility of perishing among these glorious flowers. Perhaps it was better in this beautiful place than in the river or a DP camp?

While meditating thus, I stretched myself on top of these shrubs which only slightly gave way under the weight of my body – it was like a heavenly cradle. An hour's rest gave me new strength to go on with the struggle downhill for another hour or so and in due course I saw the path! Of course, I missed the last bus and had to walk all the way to the town and the hostel. As I had never been late returning home, my absence was already causing concern. I really do not know how I managed to overcome the great exhaustion to get back; perhaps, after all, it was better to live in this ugly world than to come to a beautiful, though not very heroic, end?

No exciting news waited for me "at home" this time; but as life never goes straight but rather in a zig-zaggy way, the good luck seemed to be moving forward. My English guardian angel (my future sister-in-law Muriel) was not discouraged by our first misfortune with the visa and was determined to succeed in the end, in spite of the stiff regulations of her country, which all of those concerned wished to respect. She set a team working and with their collaboration found two jobs (for Tom and me) offered by kind people who, in the circumstances, did not insist on an interview. They were in Eire, where, fortunately, there was no need for a foreigner to work as a domestic help and remain so for four years. We would satisfy the condition of the British visitor visa to leave the country after its expiry and it would be easier to nip over from Eire than from Austria for an interview, should something more suitable turn up later.

This sounded too good to be true, and Tom and I were afraid that there might be some other hitch in Eire, preventing us from accepting the kind offer. We had almost three months' time from now to the date when we were expected to take up the appointments as teachers at two different grammar schools. In the meantime we were looking forward to getting through all the formalities involved.

There were a lot of formalities and I could not be thankful enough for my freedom from all time-consuming employments, so that I could deal with the official correspondence without delay. The academic year was finished, the University building quiet and deserted, but Tom's days and mine were filled with expectation. It was as if, all of a sudden, everything was taking a turn for the better, as if after a famine a period of plenty was approaching.

Although our Irish prospects were materially more modest than the offer from Germany, all our hearts went out to Eire; what a relief when we heard eventually from our Irish prospective employers that they had approached the authorities and had been promised that our labour permits would be issued without difficulties! Almost at the same time we had definite offers of the appointments in Germany; to the greatest surprise of Father Pierre and all the rest of the club members, we decided against the German offer, in spite of the odd chance that might still have wrecked our Irish scheme.

In the meantime British Railways decided to accept Tom, together with the Austrian students, as a seasonal worker, and sent him a copy of the labour permit to be used as a basis for his entry visa. Would it be sufficient, or would he also be accused of false pretences? The days passed, the Austrian students were ready to set off for England, but there was no sign of Tom's visa. His group left and he could do no more than wish them a pleasant journey. Naturally, he gave up all hope of his vacation enterprise in Britain.

While waiting for the Irish documents, life for the two of us became more cheerful. Tom's visa for England, to join the Austrian students, arrived after some delay, and he left me behind with a hope that I might follow shortly, too. My English patroness made a collection in her college to provide a small vacation grant for me, and when The British Federation of University Women joined in the effort, the overcautious authorities at last understood that two academic bodies should be a sufficient guarantee for a temporary admission of a frustrated refugee. I could hardly believe my eyes when my visa arrived some time in the middle of August.

The immediate problem was to make sure that I had enough money for my fare. I was saving steadily for it and the clerk at the Railway Station was kind enough to give me quotations for two routes. I could just about manage either but chose the cheaper one, even though it meant buying the ticket in three stages, thus gaining a bit through the currency exchange. In this way I could buy some food for the journey as well as keep a few shillings for an emergency.

Having sent a card to my relations in London, where I could get the very first shelter, I packed my things quickly and left the following morning, little suspecting that fate was still determined to make my desired journey an ordeal. With an immense sense of relief I watched the beautiful scenery from the train and tried to work as a communication link between the rather talkative international company in the compartment. Out of the six ladies one was Austrian, two German, one Italian, one French – and myself. The French lady said something about a strike in France, which I thought rather irrelevant as strikes in France did not concern me – but as soon as we reached the German/French border, I realized how wrong I was. Indeed, the strike did concern me, and as I was almost penniless, it concerned me more than anyone else!

The train came to a halt and did not cross the French frontier as it would normally have done. It was late in the evening on this fatal Thursday, when people looked in vain for buses or any other means of transport and when, eventually, the French lady offered to take me with her to a hotel to stay the night. I appreciated her kindness and went, having been assured by the only railwayman on duty that no trains would be available in the immediate future. We did not sleep much, and as soon as daylight broke we went to the station where my kind companion decided to take a bus to Paris. This capital was, unfortunately, off the route I had chosen in order to manage my cash, so I decided to join the crowd who were boarding a Belgian train going north. Having no Belgian visa, I had to leave the train at Metz where I realized the full value of the French art of striking. There was no train whatsoever – no use asking for one for Lille–Calais! Even the last buses disappeared by now; letter-boxes were full to the brim, letters sticking out of them and some letters were even flying about in the wind. Dustbins were not emptied and everywhere was dirty. The streets were full of curious people.

I sat in front of the station most of the day, surrounded by my two suitcases and gazed at the beautiful styles of the buildings. Then I was joined by a local middle-aged man who expressed his sympathy after he had heard about my special kind of ordeal. He offered me a huge chocolate bar which he took out of his pocket. Hesitant as I was at first to accept it, I was nevertheless very grateful for it. My own provisions were consumed by now and there was no indication of how long my journey might yet last.

Towards the evening I moved to the waiting room for the night. It was full of men of all races, mainly Algerians, people who were on the lookout as to what was to happen next, so that they could join in a riot if there was one! In a corner I saw the only two ladies in the room, a mother with her daughter, who gave me a hearty welcome in their hissing Alsatian dialect. I had never been to France before but could understand why they were so scared at the prospect of spending the night in this room, full of suspicious characters reeking of smoke and smelling of alcohol.

About midnight there was an announcement that power stations were joining in the – now general – strike. The lights went out imme-diately. In no time I felt my suitcases move. Grabbing them, I felt a hairy hand hold one of them; at the same time, my Alsatian compan-ions started screaming. I had to use my nails and feet to save my suitcases! Fortunately, the owner of the restaurant in the waiting room had the presence of mind to bring a candle; the police, too, were on the alert and came to rescue the three of us, luggage and all.

I can hardly express how glad we were to see daylight after this night. Now we could find out about our prospects of moving on. During the night, two enterprising French students came to ask if we would like to go to Paris in their minivan; I realized that Paris was nearer my destination and some better opportunity of getting on from there might be found, but I had to decline the offer as I could not afford it. Hearing my story, they were sympathetic and promised to take me for free if they collected enough people to cover the expenses. Unfortunately, they seemed to have been postponing their departure for one reason and another, so that when a holiday train bringing British holidaymakers from Switzerland appeared on the platform at about 7 a.m., I decided to join the crowd who were boarding it. The previous day, at Strassbourg, I was able to buy the second part of my ticket, i.e. for Calais, and rejoiced now to hear that this was the final destination of the train. All the seats were booked, of course, and occupied, so corridors were the only places to squeeze in. We were crowded tight, like sardines; it was almost impossible to move one's weight from one leg to the other. But it might have been possible to lift them both without falling to the floor – so crowded the train was. But at least it moved in the right direction!

But, did it? The inscriptions one could read glimpsing from the train certainly did not look French, and before long we stopped in Brussels. So, here I was, illegally on Belgian territory. No passport officers came to check on the train because they could not possibly hope to squeeze through the crowd. Perhaps my two previous illegal crossings of the border should have conditioned me for such a situation, but I was really very worried. Just now it was so vital not to get a black mark against my character! Tiredness and hunger also contributed to this state of my mind, as it was now the third day that I was on this eventful and sleepless journey.

Nothing happened until the train reached Ostend. The boat was waiting, passengers were streaming on to it and a passport officer was ticking off their documents on the board. Without the Belgian visa I hesitated to proceed with the crowd, but since the officer was on the boat itself, I had no other choice. It also meant that the boat would not leave without me, whatever happened! By now I ceased to care about anything and my only wish was to get on. Tired as I was, I could not make out which language the officer understood best; consequently, I mixed German, French and English all together, with the result that he could not understand me at all. Not only had I to tell him why I was there without a Belgian visa, but also I had to explain why I had bought a ticket only to Calais and wished to supplement it now for one for London. Such terrific economy in this situation was quite beyond the imagination of this official and his colleague who also looked at me with great suspicion. There were moments when I thought that now everything was lost, but in the end, pressed for time as the crowd behind me increased, the officer stamped an emergency visa into my travel document and did not even bother to take the fee for it.

The procedure was thus held up considerably and, by now, the boat was full. The only place I could find to sit on was the floor of the lower deck, but what did it matter now, after I had been cleared of any illegal charge or fine (would I have had to go to prison if a fine had been imposed on me and I could not pay it, I wondered) and on a boat which actually moved?

One more anxiety prevented me from dropping off to sleep as soon as I sat down on the floor next to my suitcases, namely, the passport examination at Dover. Remembering the determination of the British Consulate to bar my way to their country when I first applied for entry, I became rather apprehensive. What a surprise to find that the official was quite friendly! This event then passed as smoothly and quickly as it possibly could: obviously, I was facing an English gentleman – not a Britisher abroad.

Boarding the Dover–Victoria train, I remember a young handsome man in a Tyrolean hat decorated with jay feathers and a brush, helping me to put my suitcases on to the rack and smiling, as if he were keen on some conversation to find out who this battered creature sitting opposite might be. But as soon as I sat down, his hat and brush became rather hazy and soon disappeared. I fell asleep. A jerk at Victoria station woke me up; the Tyrolean hat appeared again, its owner was still polite and helpful, though somewhat disappointed. My eyes were now on the lookout for the signs which would lead me to my relations, who lived about twenty minutes' walk from Victoria.

With the suitcases the twenty minutes seemed very long; it did not occur to me to get a taxi even if I had had more than the few French and Austrian coins in my pocket. Following the description my relations sent me, I found their flat easily enough. It was 7.30 a.m. on Sunday (remember, I left Austria early on Thursday) and my relations, knowing about the strike in France, did not expect me yet! In fact, they were just leaving for the day to see their friends in the country. Anyway, they fed me and asked me to make myself comfortable while they were away – my need of rest was obviously showing. After a bath I slept all morning until Big Ben woke me up at noon. Was it really Big Ben? Was I not dreaming? Was it really the beginning of a new life for me, when, at last, I could live as a normal human being again? No, it was not to be – the brand of "refugee" was still to stick to me for another two years.

Chapter VI

*Vacation grant in Cambridge, but uncertainty about
the post in Eire*

Mid-August was not a good time to find academics in their customary places; soon I found that my kind friend was away from her Cambridge college for a while and that students had come back in residence for their summer vacation term, so that there was no longer a place for me. The delay caused by the lengthy visa procedure deprived me of what could have been a unique experience. The grant, of course, was available but everybody involved had already realized that it would dwindle very soon if I had to live in private accommodation. For a while, my kind relations in London, themselves refugees with a very small income, fed me, but as they lived in a very little flatlet, I had to sleep with another charitable Czech family in London. I also spent a while with my friend in Stratford-on-Avon, who treated me as her sister, but eventually the most kind-hearted family of Dr. Egon Kodíček invited me to their home after they had heard of me through The British Federation of University Women. They were actually looking for a resident domestic help, but realized my unsuitability for a permanent post of this kind already before I had arrived and the matter was not raised. They accepted me as a member of the family who would contribute to the general running of the busy household, like themselves.

It was wonderful to be treated as a human being again, no longer as a number in the official files. I was full of gratitude to all these friends that I met personally for the first time, wondering how I could return their kindness – but, can one ever repay this kind of generosity which offers not only material means but the heart as well?

Girton College gave me a very warm welcome, too, when, before long, my guardian angel returned. Feeling rather shy at first to meet such a famous scholar, I soon found myself talking to her as if we had known each other for years. Both of us rejoiced that the immense trouble she had taken on my behalf – a stranger to her up to that day – was crowned with success at last. Now, it was up to me to show that I was worthy of such sacrifices on her part, a challenge which I was longing to take.

As a friend of Professor Vočadlo, she was very interested in his fate after the communists dismissed him from Prague University, as well as in his students and their poor prospects in the totalitarian state. Our long discussions often took a turn to personal matters which brought us closer together. How modest she was about her academic achievements! Once, in the lovely garden of my hosts, she spoke about her family. "I have three brothers, one still single," she told me gently, raising her voice to stress the last part of the information. Apparently, the subject of this reference was not far from us. As a lecturer at the University College of North Wales, her youngest brother, Frank, spent his vacations mostly in Cambridge, attracted by the presence of his sister as well as by the splendid University library. Just as kind as his sister, he invited me for lunch and showed me round the library. Later, letters and occasional gifts of books from him followed – but more events took place in my life before my guardian angel and I became sisters-in-law.

The University library was now my daily abode as I tried to read all the books which were not available to me in Prague. The feeling of freedom and security was tremendous at this time, although this proved rather premature. Tom was working hard as a porter for British Railways, which made me feel almost guilty, but my instinct told me that this beautiful time could not last, that leaner days were yet to come, even if the prospect of teaching in Eire looked like a bright star on our horizon.

What a strange sensation it was to imagine oneself teaching in a foreign language! Would the Irish children laugh at my accent? Would I be able to keep my authority over them? Our labour permits had not arrived yet; Irish officials seemed to be on holiday and some delay was to be expected. In the absence of the person who was best acquainted with our case, his young and not very well informed deputy decided to act and even make "patriotic" decisions: these two people from behind the Iron Curtain might be communists and spies – surely, they must not be admitted to Eire?

So, after a double screening in Austria and a stay in Britain where our good intentions and integrity had been made abundantly clear, our labour permits and consequently entry visas to Eire were bluntly refused. This was a great shock for the two of us as well as for our friends. Their strenuous charitable work on our behalf was crumbling, after the most difficult hurdle seemed to have been overcome. What was to be done?

Letters of appeal were sent to Eire in the hope that the decision was not final; but what if it was? Our British visas were valid only for three months after which we were expected and prepared to leave the country; I am sure that the British authorities did not care whether we left for Eire or Austria, but since Eire seemed to be closed now, Austria was the only country that would receive us whether they liked it or not. What a horrid thought: to have to return to our jail from which we had emerged after so much trouble! Do recaptured prisoners feel like that? I wondered. And what if Austria rejected us? It could not, we concluded. According to the post-war agreements Austria was one of the three countries of the so called "first refuge" (Germany and Italy being the other two) and had to accept refugees before they emigrated. It seemed to me rather hard on Austria, which was occupied in an almost similar way as Czechoslovakia, that it should be punished, among other measures, by the compulsory acceptance of all the refugee "rejects".

Yet, it was clear to us that, if we had to return to Austria, getting out of it again would be very much more difficult than the first time. One would think that, perhaps, the validity of our British visas could be extended and that, in the meantime, we could find suitable jobs in Britain, but we could not ignore the fact that our visitor visas did not allow us to look for work in the country. The charge of false pretences would be imposed only too readily and justly and a pretext to banish us from the country forever might easily thus be found.

Tom's case looked easier than mine, for he entered Britain as a temporary labourer; should British Railways agree to employ him on a more permanent basis, the problem could be solved. There was some hope in his case, but my vacation grant could not be extended. Although my kind hosts were ready to make my stay with them official by describing me as their domestic help, they themselves understood that I would have hesitated to commit myself for four years; this regulation would, no doubt, apply.

All this took place at the end of August 1953; the respective grammar schools in Eire expected us on the 7th of September – too soon for us to hope to get the necessary documents in time. Tom extended his working contract with British Railways easily enough and I did my best to make myself as useful as possible to my kind hosts who had never made me feel that I had overstayed my welcome. But the validity of my visa was running out and a reason for its extension had to be found. While my learned friend still hoped to get a favourable reply from Eire, she could not be absolutely certain and decided that extenuating circumstances must allow me to take a temporary job to make my stay legal. Consequently, soon afterwards, I travelled some sixty miles north from Cambridge for an interview at an Anglo-Catholic boarding school.

The Sister Superior was kindness and sweetness itself; even if I never in the past imagined myself teaching infants, I felt that life with a person like this would sweeten every bitter pill. She made me stay overnight so that I could see the complete daily routine. It did not seem difficult, except for the compulsory silence during breakfast, resulting in the sisters' communicating with each other by very picturesque gesticulation and mimicking. It amused me at first, but no doubt in time I would be able to master this new foreign language.

Negotiations for my labour permit started immediately, but before anything could be resolved, the labour permit from Eire came, accompanied by a brief apology for the misunderstanding on the part of the writer's colleague. I felt very disloyal towards the kind Sister Superior when I wrote to her to explain my earlier commitment to Eire, but it was now something definite and could be more permanent if need be. Indeed, it was now imperative for me to leave Britain after the three months as promised, if ever I was to return there. Little did I think then that my unused application for the post at the Anglo-Catholic school would be registered in my official files and bring me later what I feared most – the accusation of false pretences.

Chapter VII

Eire

The first rays of the morning sunshine shone brightly on the boat carrying, among other travellers, two Czech refugees to the promised land. No wonder that, after fourteen months of turbulent life of insecurity, the beautiful Emerald Isle appeared to us as such. All went smoothly, but no sooner did we find ourselves in the streets than the sun hid itself behind a cloud and sent us a brisk shower – as if to refresh us after the night's travel as well as to warn us about how capricious the weather can be in this part of the world. The sun was shining again when Tom and I had to part because my school was north of Dublin, his to the south.

The Emerald Isle lived up to its name: there were large green double-decker buses, green letter boxes, green dresses on ginger-haired young Irish women, lots of green signposts and inscriptions; street names were in two languages, but the top ones, in Erse, did not seem to be noticed much. Brandishing my little textbook of Irish language, I enquired how to find my way; the kind informant did not think very much about the utility of my textbook and even less of the necessity to learn this intricate language. The streets were full of people, shop windows full of stuff for sale, but for all its busy life the place seemed to me remote, as if at the end of the world. Everything looked even more different than in England to a person of Central European mentality like myself.

It seems ridiculous now, but I cannot forget my fright on the train as it was heading north. First, round the bay, then amidst beautiful lush pastures, but then it seemed as if we were running right into the sea! Sea on the left, sea on the right, while our train was gliding briskly as if on top of all these immense waters. No sound indicating a bridge and yet, we were *not* drowned! Only after my panic had subsided, did I remind myself of all the good advice my English friends gave me. I might hear fiery, nationalist, perhaps anti-British speeches: yes, I did hear some, but much later; my future headmaster who met me at the station certainly had not prepared anything of that sort for my welcome. Neither was he capable of it: he was a very gentle, kind, elderly white-haired and broad-shouldered gentleman, with a sweet smile on his face. What a difference! I remembered a few headmasters from my school days: they seemed so stern in order to impose authority, while this one looked so friendly and human! A member of the Society of Friends, he and his wife participated in many local charities. In his goodness, he also believed that the child was born good and its natural liveliness should not be interfered with too much. The spirit of Rousseau and practical Christianity prevailed in the school – but it took a while before I could fully experience all this, including the drawbacks.

In my homeland boarding schools hardly existed. To live entirely in the school was new to me and seemed advantageous: a lot of time could be saved and given to study instead of toing and froing between home and school. However, my enthusiasm for boarding schools eventually faded and later made my departure easier, without tears.

On my way from the station the headmaster gave me a lot of useful information: his grammar school, one of the few Protestant ones in the Catholic Eire, had about fifty pupils; it was founded in the seventeenth century and had a good reputation. Across the river, in the village of Mornington, reputedly (and let the historians prove or disprove!) the Duke of Wellington was born and came on his donkey to this grammar school; the old town gate is dated from the ninth century. Not far from the town there is the famous battlefield of the Boyne. The headmaster also told me about the two wings in the school – one for the boys, the other for girls – with a classroom in-between. There was also a good swimming pool, but the school could do with a substantial grant for repairs and improvements. And, yes, my Presbyterian church could be found just round the corner near the school. Only very few pupils belonged to this Church – the majority were Church of Ireland or Methodist.

My bedsitter was not ready yet, so I was put up for the first night in a large guest-room where repairs were to be carried out soon – or so the headmaster hoped. Virginia creeper decorated the windows: just like my old home! During the night I was alarmed by a chip of plaster which fell on my face. To a person like myself, born and bred in a family house built solidly with walls like a small fortress, this more than three hundred year-old school necessarily seemed like a shell whose days were numbered – but I'm sure, it still stands there, if it survived the countless running up and down the stairs of the lively Irish teenagers. Not only the stamping of the feet made the place shake; the ceiling could also vibrate when the robust Irish terrier of the house carried out his daily ritual of scratching himself! He was a very handsome animal, more intelligent than his playful female companion; I mention this not only because I love animals, but because these two dogs belonged to school life just as much as the agile pupils, the handsome wife of the headmaster, the cat trio in the kitchen, Irish stew on Wednesdays for lunch and the bust of the Duke of Wellington in the place of honour in the dining hall.

This very bright and large dining room may not differ much from other school refectories except for the bust and another ornament, which deprived me of one of my great illusions. Under a glass lid, there was a large stuffed bird, a kind of huge goose, with a brown head and wings; I thought it was put into the dining room because it took too much space in the school's nature collections, but, alas, the school did not possess such collections – the bird was, in fact, a noble albatross. Heaven knows which poet misled me in the belief that the albatross was beautifully snow-white. Perhaps its majesty lay in its elegant, gracious flight – which this dead specimen could not exhibit for me.

Somehow, I keep on postponing my account of the Irish pupils. Yes, indirectly, they drove me out from Eire, the country of beautiful nature, lush greenery and ever so kind people. I was expected to teach French, English and European history in three forms. One had about 20 ten-to-twelve-year-olds, the second about 14 thirteen-to-fourteen-year-olds and the remaining one had only 5 fifteen-year-olds.For the first few days they saw me as an exotic creature and expected, full of curiosity, what I might be telling them; in fact, their behaviour looked promising. But, soon enough, I found that these teenagers were as if made of snakes' tails; it was a great art to keep them sitting those forty minutes of each lesson. How was it possible that in my short teaching career during the war I had no difficulty in managing a class of 60 fourteen-year-old boys and here I was baffled by 5?

It was due not so much to my foreign accent, but rather their eagerness to show off. As they were used to expressing themselves freely, heated arguments would arise, for example, mixing such different reigns of Charles IV with Charles V, making the two rulers turn in their graves as our precious time was wasted by my efforts to impose some order.

The arch-enemy of all the staff was Elaine, a thirteen-year-old chubby girl at her most awkward pubertal stage. As a recent newcomer to the school, she was bored with lessons, so she distracted everybody by her chatter. Our rebukes resulted only in her impudent answers. Once I had to expel her out of the classroom, little suspecting that this would make the situation worse. Elaine shouted while she was getting roller skates out of the cupboard in the corridor, and incited the pupils in the classroom to join her. I never realized how noisy roller skates could be; in Elaine's hands they became infernal instruments used for banging at the doors and eventually for being thrown into the window. Was it still possible to avoid using force – and was I strong enough to tame this wild animal? Shortly before the bell rang, a window was shattered; just as I was getting into the yard, the headmaster himself was already taking action. Very upset, he held the defiant Elaine by the hair while his other hand tried to retrieve the other roller skate from her grasp. He took her to his study and nobody knew what happened there. He never discussed disciplinary measures with the staff – and Elaine did not boast on this occasion.

My colleagues had similar difficulties while she was settling down to some routine in the school, but how surprisingly well all this ended! After a while Elaine fell in love with one of the older boys; this rather dull, fairly good-looking student hardly realized how, unwittingly, he turned this little dragon into a lamb. Elaine took to her study and was showing ability; her good ideas were just as original as her previous, outrageous ones. When the headmaster asked me if I would be willing to give piano lessons to a few pupils, Elaine was the most enthusiastic. Believe it or not, we became friends and she used me as a confidante; I do not know how her Andy responded in the end, but can only wish them both all the best.

Disorderly behaviour of this degree was, of course, an exception, but there was no lack of distracting elements among the pupils. Some of them abused the headmaster's kindness, making the work of the teachers difficult. Yet, unused as I was to life in a boarding school, I was agreeably surprised at how friendly the staff and students could be outside the teaching hours. Lots of activities were practised: swimming, chess, music, model-making, gardening, handicrafts. When a few girls asked me to teach them how to crochet, they managed it much quicker than learning ten French words. In this situation it was not surprising that the pupils invited me to join them on Sunday afternoons for bicycle trips and borrowed the necessary vehicle for me from someone very quickly. Perhaps a child *is* born good, after all, but only as long as you do not try to teach it? Yes, a lot can be learnt in a boarding school unobtrusively in one's spare time.

Most of my colleagues were resident, too, and all very nice. I had a great respect for the main teacher of English, a middle-aged lady and the best disciplinarian of all of us; I also remember a rather phlegmatic colleague who was a secret communist (the party was forbidden in Eire).In his idealism he seemed to have suffered from a kind of mild persecution mania and a resulting martyr-like reticence. In contrast, there was a young, pretty, energetic matron who taunted the men and had a much more direct and effective method of education than the headmaster's good words: she rightly reckoned that the pupils would not boast about the special treatment by hand that they were getting in her office. I also remember the tiny, deft-handed cook who had to work hard, preparing all the meals. I do not know why people tend to grumble at institutional food; for me, who, not so long ago, had to swallow the tasteless polenta, the school meals seemed to me good, nourishing and adequate, although I do remember the sausages from the local pepper-loving butcher, which made our mouths burn. I remember also the nice Sunday lunch jelly which was new to me. I can still see it quivering on the spoon held by the headmaster's trembling hand, watched intently by so many eyes, including mine, lest the blob would miss the plate. It must have been a great relief for the kind man when this ritual was over. A few times, on Sundays, he took me with his wife, daughter and the dogs for walks on the beach: the majestic sea was still a great mystery for me.

On other Sunday afternoons I explored the town and its surroundings, either with a few pupils or alone. I also read a lot, not only my favourite literature, but Irish dramatists, poets, history and mythology: what a wealth of imagination there is in literature! Sunday evenings I was expected in the Presbyterian church to accompany the hymns on the harmonium. After the service there was a pleasant moment or two spent in the manse with the minister and his wife. Sometimes an elderly gentleman joined us. He was ninety-two, but still fit enough to walk the distance about half-a-mile between the church and his home. He lived alone and was glad to receive visitors, so that I had yet another place to go on occasion.

As Christmas was approaching, an invitation for Tom and myself came from my Stratford friend and was gratefully accepted. Although my salary was small, the free board and lodgings allowed me to save enough for such a journey, even for a few presents for our host and her family. As she knew our native country and my mother, to be with her was the nearest we could get to our home, although, of course, my mother and brother were very much on my mind. Christmas celebrations in England seemed so much more lavish than our Christmas Eve carp and sweets, carols, modest presents and Christmas tree. Compared with the war-time blackout and dim lighting under the communists, the bright lights of Stratford and Birmingham nearly dazzled us. But what an end to such a pleasant holiday! On our return journey a great storm tossed the boat on the angry sea in the Irish Channel, letting me sample seasickness in full!

The two sea channels between the European Continent and Eire made me wonder how much information about the rest of the world could reach ordinary people. Irish politics was beyond my under-standing; how was it possible that, not so long ago, the lights of Dublin were allowed to guide Hitler's bombers towards their targets on the western side of England? Did the Irish really sympa-thize or did they prepare an alibi should one be needed? Once I met a well educated official whose unawareness surprised me: as I was referred to as a refugee from Czechoslovakia, he thought I must be one of those poor Sudeten Germans, driven out of their homes after the war! My purely Czech origin did not impress him and the fact that, for the last four years my country had had a totalitarian communist government under which democratically-minded people were not safe, sounded surprising to him.

There was one memorable event in the school life I experienced. Just before Easter, the pupils were to leave for their break on the 1st of April, the day when any prank may be tolerated. Address labels on pupils' suitcases ready for transport home were changed, pictures in classrooms misplaced, the poor terrier bitch was howling locked in the coal house, a white chamber pot was swung on the bell tower and the Duke of Wellington's bust disappeared from its usual place in the hall. Who could have moved such a heavy object? The only culprits could have been the oldest, strongest boys, sensible enough to return it after the break. But no, they swore innocence on their return, so that theft was the only explanation. Strange that a burglar set his heart on this heavy object of no great artistic value and nothing else?

About six weeks later the mystery deepened. The school's maintenance officer came across the bust in a nearby pub, soiled beyond recognition by the mud of the river from where local fishermen had pulled it out with great difficulty. After having been carefully cleaned at the school, the Duke regained his previous likeness, except for a black moustache which he seemed to have acquired during his banishment. It was tar, stuck so firmly in position that it could not be removed for some time. No Sherlock Holmes was at hand to offer an explanation, but it looked like a case of patriotic revenge on a compatriot who – so long ago! – had sold his soul to the British. Clearly, such "political" acts took place here with impunity in 1954.

During the Easter holiday I treated myself by going to explore this beautiful country. I had already visited Dublin several times, on the invitation of my Irish guardian angel, Muriel's friend Jocelyn, Professor of History at Trinity College, Dublin. She introduced me to the most important libraries where I spent many happy hours. This time she took me to Wicklow and Glendaloch, with its dreamy lake, ancient church with the slim round tower in an almost perfect condition in spite of its age of about 1,000 years, and the rock with St. Kevin's bed – all surrounded by magnificent forests on the slopes. How clever were these hermits to find such lovely places for their prayers! The Irish were rightly proud of their early Christian tradition and some insisted that hermits could still be found. Believe it or not, I met one, in the very south of Eire where, staying in a YWCA hostel, I spent a few days of that same Easter holiday. One of Tom's colleagues, a teacher of Irish, took us for a long walk – and there the hermit was: huddled at the far end of a very primitive dwelling built of stones and tree branches, in complete darkness so that he was hardly visible. Eventually, the sound of the Irish language from our leader coaxed him out. Dirty and unkempt as he was, his clothes indicated some contact with human civilization; in Irish, he intimated that he used to be in the army and now had a small pension, enough to live on in this manner. Annoyed that he had been found, he intended to move – but that could have been only an excuse to prevent further visitors from coming. I am sure he did not fill his time with praying; although he must have had some reason for his aversion towards people, our guide thought that he sneered at the comforts of civilized life because they had to be paid for by work and effort.

Feeling guilty having trespassed on this individual's wish for solitude, I also realized how relaxed the life in this end-of-the-world island was, compared with the bustling European continent. Dublin was an exception, but nobody seemed to be in a hurry in the provinces. When I came to collect my repaired shoes at the appointed time, they were far from ready. The cobbler had promised because he wanted to please me; now, he was offering me a chair and, while repairing my shoes, he entertained me with umpteen stories so that I did not count the time. What a fantasy! No, he would not speed up his work, but I could imagine him singing when alone and taking pride in his honest toil.

The Easter break passed quickly and I was back at the school. It is not necessary to stress my pleasure at being in frequent corre-spondence with my friends and relatives in England; but unfortunately, no direct contact with my mother could be estab-lished. She, as well as my brother and a few other relatives, had been interrogated by the police for a long time after my escape and one should not make the situation worse for them by trying to contact them. Only my Stratford friend could smuggle a few secret messages from me to my mother into her letters to her relatives in Czechoslovakia and vice versa. We missed each other very much indeed, but as things stood we had to accept the possibility, even probability, that we would not see each other again. If, at least, I could prove to my mother that I was on the right path, that my escape *did* make sense . . .

My greatest ambition was to find a place in a British institution to achieve equal qualifications with British subjects of the same status. Although my Prague doctorate was fully respected, it was a foreign paper of a foreign speaker, offering thus only limited chances when applying for posts. On my way to visit the elderly gentleman whom I met at church attendance, I used to call at the public library and also bought *The Times Literary Supplement* where various grants and scholarships were advertised. But there were not many available, I am sorry to say: British undergraduates were getting their grants from their local authorities; foreign students were supported by their governments; only specialized studentships appeared occasionally; but, mostly, stateless people were not eligible. And then a letter came from Cambridge, written in an unfamiliar handwriting: Muriel, my guardian angel, had been taken seriously ill and should not be contacted until further notice. No more details were given, and only every now and then did I hear from her colleagues or her brother about the slow progress towards her recovery.

Sad and worried, I sent off one or two applications without much hope for success. But then, not long after Easter, a notice in *TLS* struck me: the newly established research studentship at Oxford, with all its conditions, seemed tailor-made for me. The applicant should be a woman (St. Hugh's College being a women's college then), with a degree from a Czechoslovak, Polish or Oxford university, ready to spend a year working for a diploma in Czech, Slovak or Polish studies; the grant was renewable for another year, should the need arise. This sounded too good to be true! Countless disappointments put me on my guard not to get my hopes raised too much; yet, however disloyal to my kind headmaster I felt, I sent my application without delay. Could such an opportunity be missed?

What a thrill to be invited for an interview, even if it meant travelling by overnight boat both ways in succession and then straight into the classroom. Apart from myself there was another interviewee, a young Oxford graduate who, I thought, would stand a better chance. Yet, I felt an immediate rapport with the chairman of the committee. It was the unforgettable Professor of Comparative Slavonic Philology, Boris O. Unbegaun himself who congratulated me shortly afterwards when he told me that I was to be the first holder of the Rawnsley Studentship.

My joy was marred only by the impossibility of sharing it with my mother and my dear friend in Cambridge who was still in seclusion, though well on the way to recovery. No doubt, she suspected a perennial student in me from the start – how glad she would be now. But back to reality, for I had to return to my Irish school for a while yet, to my chirruping pupils and the now quite pleasant Elaine. They were all busy revising for their sessional examinations as well as preparing for the sports day, which was to take place shortly before the end of the school year which ended on the 30th of June.

I had three months before my Oxford College could receive me; in fact, they had no room for postgraduates in the college buildings and I was expected to find suitable lodgings. Where could I spend the three months till October when I had to leave the school at the end of June? Temporary work was advertised, but few posts with residence which I would have preferred, however much it would have limited my freedom and privacy. That way promised more saving, so urgently needed for the next year, as my grant amounted to only a little above half of a student's regular one. While regular students could stay with their parents during vacations, I had to provide for myself for the whole year and for the college fees as well.

The kind and understanding headmaster gave me a good testimonial and, one day, a middle-aged couple came to see me: they needed a governess for their children during the long vacation who would be willing to coach their youngest, a boy of eight, every morning. There would be other staff (domestic) and I would have my own room; only, they lived in a country house surrounded by a sizeable estate, situated a few miles away from the nearest small town. Would I not miss the company of young people, dancing, pubs, the cinema? I have never danced in my life and after the busy life in the school the place seemed idyllic. I accepted and agreed to come at the end of June.

The gentleman, an army major, met me at the railway station. He had another errand that day, namely to collect another newcomer to the estate, a French poodle puppy of a noble pedigree of which he seemed very proud. The whimpering little creature shivered in her box, full of apprehension – just like me. She was my friend from the beginning, as I responded better than anyone to her playful appeals; this could happen only in secret as one could not interfere with her training. Her master's military orders only puzzled her: surely, this is not the way to treat a lady of such a noble birth like me? The master was not very pleased with his new acquisition. But this is said only in passing – for I want to return to our arrival at the estate, which was a new experience for me.

I had seen a number of country mansions in my homeland, but they were not lived in – what would this be like? I imagined almost a castle – and a castle it was, but only in the sense of "my house, my castle". A long winding lane led up the hill from the lodge towards the house: too small for my idea of a castle, too large for an ordinary house. One part of it looked rather dilapidated, but the explanation came indirectly before long: they had bought the estate only a few years ago and were gradually repairing and refurbishing the house; it was slow progress because they did not live there all the year round. The potential expense was beyond my imagination, but it appeared that even limited means enabled the purchase of a neglected country house in Eire for those who liked to live a genteel life. I did not count the rooms – there could have been as many as thirty, but only about one-third were habitable. My pleasant room looked out onto the lush lawn, perhaps rather a pasture with cows and sheep, and on a lot of trees. It was very quiet.

The lady of the house was a real Lady: daughter of a late Admiral, she was very kind, fair and understanding, without any sign of class haughtiness or pride in her manner. She introduced me to the domestic staff and the children when they eventually came from their respective schools in England for their long vacation. The eldest daughter was nearly twenty, a student at an art school; her Etonian brother was seventeen, so they would not expect much help from me, except, perhaps, occasional company. My main duties would be with the thirteen-year-old Janet and eight-year-old Jamie, who were the last to come from their public schools. We had barely two months to catch up with what young Jamie failed to learn at school, but he much preferred play to learning – and was particularly fond of the French poodle puppy. He loved fairy tales and grasped some knowledge through them, but how could one teach Latin grammar through play? My copy of Comenius' *Orbis Pictus* was somewhere in my Czech home (or was it? – the communists may have confiscated my complete library?); ordinary picture books helped to learn Latin words, but what about grammar, such as it was for the eight-year-olds? Grammar was taught in public schools and one could have lost one's place in the school if one failed the examinations. Latin grammar was vital for young Jamie, who only came to life in the afternoons or weekends when there were games, walks, and occasional car drives with or without swimming in the beautiful clear sea. What fun we had on the walk to a place of pilgrimage, with Jamie's new camera! He was so excited that, before anyone could show him how to focus, his camera swinging on his chest was clicking as he was ruining his first film. Needless to say his military father was not amused and gave a resentful look to the governess.

However, I think I must have lost this gentleman's respect

already before this event; the unfortunate *bouquet garni* had caused that when the great house party was being prepared. I had never been to a big party before and thought that they existed only in Jane Austen's novels; now, I was actually to see one. The major did not mind driving 150 miles to Dublin to get the best salmon, meats, wine and numerous delicacies unavailable in the vicinity of the estate. Waiters were hired and the cook got extra help in the kitchen for the occasion. The major himself conducted the operations, choosing the dishes from a cookery book; I had to translate the French recipes, but, alas, when I did not know what *bouquet garni* consisted of in the culinary sense, his contemptuous look indicated that the last bit of his regard for my education was lost – if he ever had any.

I did not expect to be invited to the party and the débâcle with the *bouquet garni* increased my hope that I would not, but, alas, in the middle of the bustle my well-meaning lady came to see me, taking it for granted (and she was right) that I would not possess a long evening dress. Would I go upstairs with her to choose one. My heart sank; what did I know about fashion, evening wear in particular? Something black, ill-fitting and uncomfortable was put on me and was approved of, as nothing more suitable was found among the family cast-offs. So, there I was, feeling like Fanny in *Mansfield Park*, only, instead of her Portsmouth family, my own in Czechoslovakia as well as those in Displaced Persons' camps were on my mind. Only Jane Austen could reconcile such diverse worlds satisfactorily – when the evening approached, I must have looked so miserable that the good hostess conceded that I need not take part if I did not want to.

So, I did not see the great party in the superbly decorated ground floor rooms and eat at the beautiful table in the dining room. This elegant piece of furniture stays in my memory. The major was rightly proud of it: it was very long and narrow and had a little mouse carved on one of the legs as a trade mark. Normally, the family took all meals at this table, the master and mistress at each end of it. When eventually all the young members of the family were back at their schools and I was left in the middle of the table between the parents, I had a lot of exercise getting up and down again during the meals as dishes needed to be passed from one end to the other.

The company of the two elder siblings gave me a lot of pleasure, the Etonian being particularly nice. They knew very little about the communist world or the reasons why people ran away from it and asked me all sorts of questions. As young people do, they left their parents to travel or visit, returning back when the money had run out. Once or twice the parents, too, left for a few nights, leaving the cook and myself in charge of the house and the two youngest children. No sooner had the parents disappeared than the pubertal young lady sneered at my authority. In an army style like her father's, she ordered us about as well as the rest of the staff, perhaps just to occupy herself; but her waywardness could never equal Elaine's. We made peace when walking the dogs: the French poodle, although now more civilized, was still slipping out of control, while the cute elk-spitz showed gracious good sense, but no army order from the girl would move the fat, dim spaniel to a brisker pace.

There was not much spare time during the first two months, but in September, after the young people returned to their schools, I was left almost redundant. The lady of the house always had small jobs for me, but I had enough time to see to all the formalities connected with my transfer to England. With a grant from an Oxford college the door to England was open to me at last! And what was more: a letter came from Cambridge, written by Muriel herself who, with her health restored, was back to work. She congratulated me sincerely on my success. No doubt, I would be able to see her again soon.

My good lady herself supervised her children's packing and preparations before their departure; the holiday was now over for the time being and she reminded me that I, too, was going to "school" and what about my wardrobe? By now I had quite a good collection of well preserved clothes given to me by kind ladies I met along my odyssey. Among them were two camisoles from an old lady (or so she seemed to me, although she may not have been much over sixty), which I should have kept as a souvenir; they would be valuable museum pieces! However, with some alterations carried out by hand in my time off I could see myself as quite well dressed among the Oxford students. The lady decided that I should have new shoes. In the same way as she did for her own children, she bought me a pair of sandals and a pair of walking shoes which I was allowed to choose. The sandals were red, I remember, the lace shoes black; as we walked home on the pathway, the sun-lit banks of heather in full bloom looked even more beautiful than on normal days.

As the time of my departure was approaching, I had to find out how to leave this place. I am sure it is very different now, but in those days transport was rather limited. Sunday rest was strictly observed, leaving bus and rail stations locked up so that one could not even look up the timetable for Monday travel. Only footballers and their fans could go by hired coaches to play or see the matches, so I was told, but for that sort of travel I would not qualify. The nearby small town was situated on the Waterford–Cork line, but the train went only once a day, leaving Waterford in the morning and returning from Cork in the evening. So I could visit Cork on one of my days off, but could not do the same with Waterford, unless I was ready to do the sight-seeing during the night. One of my local informants was almost offended when I doubted about a morning coach connection to Waterford: "Of course there is!" he insisted. Thus reassured I took his advice, little suspecting that changing the coach and waiting for the connection for several hours meant nothing to him. Although I left for Waterford in the morning, I reached it in the evening, just in time for the Rosslare–Fishguard overnight boat.

Tom came from Waterford to wish me well and wave me goodbye. He was not so lucky as to get a university grant, but a men's Oxford college accepted him as a postgraduate student, with special permission to work his way through as a librarian; so, he would follow me before long. The sponsorship of the two Oxford colleges, at last, made the British authorities allow us to stay in the country for at least a year; even so, being stateless, we had to report to the police every six months.

My Rawnsley Studentship amounted to £200 per annum. It seemed a fortune to an impecunious refugee like myself, although local authorities routinely awarded £350 a year to their students who were expected to depend on their parents during vacations. However, it was quite common for students in Prague to earn their living in the course of their studies; I was hoping to supplement the studentship in a similar way. This, unfortunately, was not allowed to College grant holders; so, I paid £80 for the College fees and wondered how far the remainder would cover my expenses, especially for the private lodgings. Within the regulations which the College had to observe, they were very helpful. Soon enough I was moving to a very nice flat of a tutor who, for health reasons, wished to have a mature student living with her; she took me in for a nominal rent and the College gave me free lunches. This was paradise!

The hungry days in the DP camps were long forgotten and the Irish wholesome, frugal meals seemed monotonous in comparison with the College food. The cooks were delighted to see me accepting gratefully second helpings of their delicious puddings which were sneered at by some students. In fact, it seemed to me that those who did not criticize college food were not considered refined enough. I could not agree and, moreover, could not really afford to be so refined: the second helping kept the wolf away for the rest of the day – a welcome saving.

Friendships were soon made, not only with students, but also with tutors who had nothing to do with my subject – what a pleasant, homely atmosphere! Already during the first interview I suggested that I would like to work on the literary relationship of the modern Czech classic writer Karel Čapek with English writers. My supervisor gave me complete freedom of choice within the subject; the Bodleian and the Taylorian libraries became my daily abode. Consultations with my supervisor, mostly in his home, were something to look forward to, especially after he told me that he knew my Prague supervisor, Professor O.Vočadlo: they had met in Buchenwald concentration camp during the war, where, together with other prisoners, they held secret Byzantino-Slavic seminars on Sundays. Alas, on weekdays, they were made to remove dead bodies . . .

By Christmas I could submit my first substantial written piece of work. Professor Unbegaun considered it suitable as part of a D.Phil. thesis and suggested a transfer from the diploma to the higher degree. This meant that the studentship, renewable for one more year according to the regulations, could be extended: one more year in England for a stateless person! Of course, applications had to be made, but the college Principal's unwavering support at last persuaded the authorities that I was no parasite and should be allowed to stay indefinitely. What a weight off my shoulders! Tom was now in Oxford, too, working on his D.Phil. thesis as well as being a librarian. Owing to this double workload he needed a bit longer to finish his thesis than I did, but the goal was eventually reached and he was lucky to get a post at an important university in the north of England.

Already in my second year the Rawnsley Studentship was increased to £300 (it now stands at £5,455!). It meant the end of my good free lunches and the beginning of a more frugal diet (fish and chips cost then 1/6d, 1lb of cheddar cheese 2/6d) on which my body and spirit were thriving equally well. At the end of the second year my thesis was nearly finished. I had no problem to complete it soon afterwards, even if the grant could not be extended any more. But a Prince Charming (who soon became my husband) appeared on the scene at the right time and carried me away to beautiful North Wales, not on a splendid white steed, but by train, leaving Euston station at about 4 p.m. So ended my Oxford fairy tale, only to initiate a new one, leading to my academic career.

Reckoning

Chapter VIII

Happy marriage, but communist régime still imposes its
power
Conclusion

Perhaps my story should end here for, indeed, my husband and myself were happy ever after – and I ceased to be a stateless person. Life should be normal as I became a member of a kind, loving and respected family; in many ways it *was* normal – only my own kin were far away, behind the impenetrable Iron Curtain. For many years, every now and then, my anxiety for them brought about in my dreams the image of a communist policeman, the feared and ruthless STB, walking on the path round my native house, but I dare say that now the régime did not waste their spying on a person like me any longer; once they saw that I was no dangerous political animal who might upset their rule, they seemed to have lost interest. My marriage to a British subject reassured them, although clearly their grudge caused by my obvious disapproval of them had not been forgotten.

Direct correspondence between my mother and other relations and friends was now possible without exposing them to the danger of persecution, provided we were cautious, as strict censorship still posed a threat. Parcels were allowed, but they were censored too: although no sensible Czech letter writer would have dared to complain about the great shortages in the country, we knew about them from the media and could fill our parcels accordingly. Second-hand clothing was more likely to reach its destination than new things. Books were usually delivered, provided you avoided sending anything politically "offensive". A Bible would be confiscated immediately, as would a valuable dictionary: why should an individual (even a specialist who needed the dictionary) enjoy the ownership of a book if it could serve *all* in a depleted institutional library? In this way our many gifts to friends were officially stolen.

Every time I went shopping and saw an elderly woman shuffling along with her little shopping bag, in my mind's eye I saw my mother queuing for hours for a piece of meat, a reel of cotton, a couple of ugly brown oranges from Cuba, or any incredibly common trifle – queuing perhaps in vain as the desired article was sold out before her turn came.

Every now and then the régime reminded me of their power to inflict pain and spoil my happiness. My brother in Prague still kept his post at the institute for literature (although his salary ceased to be increased) because he was needed there, but he had to experience seeing his two gifted sons being refused entry to grammar school. They became apprentices in factories instead. What a waste of talent, and all because their intellectual parents did not sing the right political tune. Obviously, the boys were to make up for their non-conforming parents; as menial workers they could study in their spare time and sit the final grammar school examinations eventually, to qualify for university. They graduated successfully in spite of the added compulsory effort.

The sixties brought some relief. The communist cage opened its door for Professor Vočadlo who was allowed to attend the Shakespeare anniversary celebrations in 1964, and visited us on the same occasion; my close friend, from the days of our university studies, now teacher of English in Prague, came to practise her English. Another dear "college" friend visited us – and then the miracle happened: my mother was granted permission to visit us in 1964 and two years later, to move to us for good; never mind that she had to give up her pension and property and promise never to return! What a joy for us! Can you imagine a lady of eighty-three who had never travelled in a plane and hardly spoke any English taking such a decision? Yes, there she was then, at Heathrow, among the last people getting through the controls because she could not easily communicate with the officials. In her hands she held all her property squeezed into a small suitcase and a hold-all, while her now weakened eyes searched anxiously for the daughter whom she had not seen for twelve years. We almost made up for the lost time, as she lived with us until her death at the age of ninety-four.

My mother loved my husband dearly – which he appreciated,

having lost his own parents rather early (father at 11, mother at 17); she communicated with him in German, but by listening she learnt enough English to get the gist of our conversation in English. But there was hardly anyone among our friends who could talk to her more effectively in Czech or German. She wrote countless letters to her son and friends in Czechoslovakia, but for live conversation there was practically just myself. I did my best to satisfy her curiosity as everything was so very new to her, but it was not always easy to "connect", as E. M. Forster would describe the situation. By now I had come to terms with my illusion that the best way of making myself useful to both my old and new countries would be through teaching my native Czech language, literature and general European culture. But who would like to learn it in Britain if there was no practical use, hardly any contact with the country, with even the beauty of Prague disappearing under the grubbiness of the régime's neglect? It was one of the greatest surprises in my life that actually my other subject, English literature (later combined with Education), gave me a career full of pleasure and satisfaction. With little confidence at first I worked hard to bring myself on a par with my British-born colleagues, an activity which did not always mix too well with the need to entertain my mother, but the sisters Brontë and Dickens, whom she had read in translation, often provided the connecting link. She expected me to "tell my day" to her and was interested in my students. Looking back on all those years, I must have taught over a thousand students; mostly they became teachers, some remained in touch and I can only hope that our contact had added the Central European dimension to their insular horizon at the time when the Iron Curtain was separating East and West so completely.

A gradual relaxation and hope for Czechoslovakia was on the way during the Dubček era; censorship was lifted, and Czech students could take seasonal work or attend language courses in Britain. But this pleasure was short-lived as the Russians and their allies invaded their homeland in August 1968. The young people were summoned to return home; some obeyed, but others decided to stay and ask for asylum which, thank heaven, was readily granted. What new hazards were there for our nation now? During those eleven years of my mother's stay with us my brother, now widowed, could visit us several times, permission being usually given to the nearest of kin. Would we be able to see him again now? In spite of the régime becoming increasingly more restrictive, he did come, having reached pensionable age: the government would have retained his pension if he did not return . . . But he would not give them that advantage; he had his two sons in Prague and his institute still needed him, too. Yet, mother was not deprived of the pleasure of seeing him practically every year of her life that remained. After her death my husband and I saved my brother the arduous train journey to us by meeting him half-way: the Czechs could move fairly freely within the Eastern block, including Yugoslavia which was the land of their dreams, and it was there that we spent a happy holiday together. Who would have thought that this was the last meeting between my husband and my brother? Only a few years after mother's death my dear Frank followed her, just as we were planning our early retirement and preparing our move to Cambridge. He was so much looking forward to living in his old university city, but it was not to be and I had to come there alone.

Grief had brought my sister-in-law and myself closer together. Cambridge was nearer to Prague than North Wales, but it still was not safe for me to visit Czechoslovakia. By now my brother's sons had finished their studies, were married and had families: would I ever meet these new relatives? I booked a hotel for my brother and myself in Dresden where my British citizenship would be respected and where at least one of my nephews could bring his family over for the day. But first I had to experience the horror of getting through the Iron Curtain in Berlin . . . It began with the search through the train by uniformed men with guns, examining our luggage, looking under every seat, even bringing a ladder to make sure that no refugee was hiding on the roof – and then came the claustrophobia of the dark, short and very narrow corridor with the passport officer's grim face towering over me from behind a counter high above, almost from the ceiling . . .

But the journey was worthwhile for, apart from my brother, I *did* meet the young family as well. Their train came with a considerable delay on that cold spring day; if we wanted to speak freely, we had to avoid the hotel where secret tape recorders were almost certainly installed. So, the three little girls had to keep pace with the grown-ups, until a bench in a park gave me the first opportunity to open my bag with the presents. "Whew! Pears!!", the five voices sounded in unison. The fruit was consumed remarkably quickly. Why were pears such a high-profile merchandise in communist countries? There were plenty of pears available in my young days, but now they were probably left rotting on or under the trees. Perhaps people in the villages had some, but the pears did not get into the town shops, certainly not in the spring. Why do such trivial matters stick in one's memory, almost overshadowing the joy the time together gave us? Yet, they, too, reflect the life in the communist "paradise".

Over the next few years my brother and I spent our annual holidays together, mostly in East Germany. A few months after the last and best one, in 1988, he wrote to me that he had leukaemia and had only a few months to live. Incredulous and hopeful for some miraculous cure I suppressed the urge to go and see him, but when he was moved to hospital, I felt that I must act quickly. Of course, a visa was needed and, in my case, also an assurance of a safe return to England. Apparently, my application required a special, personal interview with the Consul. Now I was to get the full taste of the acrimonious communist bureaucracy: this was October, my brother was critically ill and the first interview the Consul could offer me was some time in the middle of January. Nothing could be done earlier. My brother died on Christmas Eve, before I could see him.

If only he could have lived a year longer, to see the freedom of his country restored! On my first journey back, after the Velvet Revolution, I saw the drabness and neglect of the precious buildings in Prague, pollution worse than I could imagine. What a waste and unnecessary misery all those long years. But the spirit of the people did not perish, even if now they are paying a heavy price for their freedom, and progress may be slower than they wish. I count my blessings that I was reunited with my mother and brother, although, initially, all this looked so hopeless.

The liberation came too late for me to show Prague to my husband; Muriel was now ageing and her infirmity did not allow her to make the journey there either. But she did rejoice with me and followed the development of the new democracy with great interest. Somehow, we felt the satisfaction for both of us that "all's well that ends well", as if those efforts she had "invested" in me in the past, had brought good results. Her physical frailty and my widowhood, and our joint presence in Cambridge brought us even closer to each other. All the more I felt the urge to look after her, but she guarded her independence, so that my part could be played only with discretion. In 1993, her sudden death shocked and grieved us all very much, but perhaps one can see some satisfaction in its suddenness, too. She would have hated lengthy lingering illness – and she was not alone (as she feared) when her hour struck: I was with her, having only just returned from a trip to America, with a report and pictures to show her.

All the years without Frank and Muriel have not weakened my bond to the rest of the Bradbrook family or to Britain. The liberation of my native country has brought back to me at least the younger generation of my growing Czech family where I feel warmly welcome. I can go and see them freely as well as the country itself whenever I wish. If only I knew the name of the village from where we started our walk "over the hills", I would like to try it again: what would it be like with a passport and without a fear of being shot? I wonder . . .

Cambridge, 2000